PLATE I

RARE HOOKED RUGS

Plate 2.
Reproduction by
Mrs. Molly Nye Tobey
of Barrington, R. I., of
a fine half-century-
old rug.

Colored materials used
were pieces from an old
woolen quilt; center background, wool from her own
sheep; the border, an old
woolen blanket dyed with
black walnut husks.

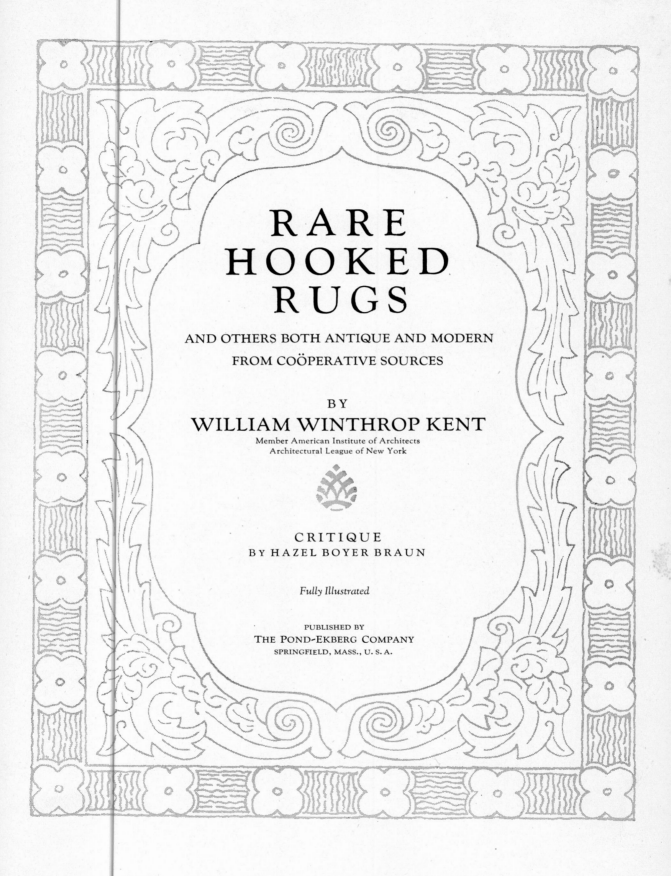

RARE HOOKED RUGS

AND OTHERS BOTH ANTIQUE AND MODERN

FROM COÖPERATIVE SOURCES

BY

WILLIAM WINTHROP KENT

Member American Institute of Architects
Architectural League of New York

CRITIQUE
BY HAZEL BOYER BRAUN

Fully Illustrated

PUBLISHED BY
THE POND-EKBERG COMPANY
SPRINGFIELD, MASS., U. S. A.

Second Printing 1948

PRINTED IN THE UNITED STATES OF AMERICA BY
THE PUBLISHERS, THE POND-EKBERG COMPANY
SPRINGFIELD, MASSACHUSETTS

TO
JESSIE ADAMS KENT
MY WIFE
AND TO OTHER MEMBERS OF THE FAMILY ACCORDINGLY
AS THEY HAVE SUFFERED, ENDURED, AND HELPED, IN
THE MAKING OF THIS LITTLE CONTRIBUTION TO HANDI-
CRAFT IN ALL COUNTRIES

CRITIQUE

"Art is called Art because it is not Nature." — GOETHE

NVENTIVE genius called into activity by man's inspirations is the wellspring of that contagious joy that artists find in their work. When this creative mind is in possession of the human faculties, the petty things of life drop away, the possibilities of ever greater achievement lift the human being to a freedom that only an artist knows.

We always find that the man or woman who turns to art after retirement from professional or business life is certain to be an enthusiastic, alert and vital person. This was one of the secrets of that true culture that old China sustained for a longer time than almost any other nation. It was, in far ancient times and in rare cases still is, the custom for a man to give a part of his life to education and to service of his country in official capacity after passing the examinations. But his thought life always includes the arts — music, poetry and painting. The fundamental ideas of Chinese religions taught that beauty is within and each must bring it out. After finishing official service with high honor, then man should turn to the arts to bring to them the richness he had gleaned in life and to fill his ripe years with that joy of creative meditation.

We thought of this recently when we studied a portfolio of designs made by William Winthrop Kent for hooked rugs. Kent

From the SAN DIEGO *(California)* TRIBUNE-SUN, *Sunday, March, 1940.*

[VII]

comes each winter to La Jolla and carries always with him a note-book in which he jots down the possibilities for a pattern. An architect of distinction, he naturally thinks in terms of structural pattern. Being a New Englander, he loved the old furniture, and the rugs they made — as they did their quilts — from scraps of material.

He noted the rugs had quaint ideas expressed in their designs, but not always were they adjusted to the material or the purpose of service. We can all remember that the housewife sometimes enjoyed sketching her favorite in the domestic animal family — the dog, the cat, or the colt, to dominate her hooked rug.

At first perhaps these were just thoughts about rugs to Kent, then he began to wonder where this art really started. Many have supposed it to be an American folk art. His research soon con-vinced him that this could not be. He traced the rug to England then started a search for its source. He found that the Copts of Egypt hooked rugs in the sixth century. He traced them back at least a hundred years in England and 400 years in Scotland. Then through an enthusiastic correspondent in Scotland (Miss Ann Macbeth, of Hartsop, Cumberland, England, and former instruc-tor of Glasgow Art School), he got trace of ancient findings of hooked blankets in Norway. At Oslo he learned that the thick piling of what they called *rye* weaving was used on the beds to take the place of furs. With the Vikings he left off and perhaps decided, as we usually do, that each art we attempt to run down disappears in the haunts of Central Asia where, some of these days, the excavations will bring to light not only the beginning of so much that we have now but evidence of greater inventions and more intelligent living than we know today.

[VIII]

In his book called *The Hooked Rug**, illustrated with 175 scholarly findings, Kent preserved his research and fine thoughts on the subject for all of us, the standard book thereon. In fact, the *Encyclopedia Britannica* lists him as the authority on the subject. But the best result of the whole interest is the fun he has all the time now, making designs for these rugs. He renders them with such completeness and care in colored crayons that each is a small work of art. The alertness for design possibilities gives an added zest to life and keeps this interest a growing thing. The Kent designs are now used for hooked rugs in China and Japan and in the modern rugs, where the planes are larger, the piling quite thick and the range of color fascinating.

His rugs form a quaint record of world travels. Perhaps the motif might have come from a tiny flower he saw on a mountainside or it might be from a Chinese painting, a Persian miniature, a mosque decoration in Constantinople, a stained glass window in Italy, an Indian basket. This love of design has led also to an interest in the backs of playing cards for The Kem Company.

We feel sure that Kent would agree with Ruskin when he said, "Design is not the offspring of idle fancy; it is the studied result of accumulative observation and delightful habit."

HAZEL BOYER BRAUN

*Dodd, Mead & Company, New York, 1930

INTRODUCTION

WHEN the late Will H. Low wrote so graciously and well the Foreword for *The Hooked Rug,* it could hardly have been anticipated that a book of that nature would have a reprinting. It was, however, so well received by those interested in the subject that a popular edition followed, which gratified both publishers and author because being less expensive than the first printing the book thus went into the hands of very many more readers. Letters in its praise were received from many sources in America, England and Australia.

In *The Hooked Rug* the origin of the method was discussed and proved to have been not American nor English, but Scandinavian, or from some prehistoric source antedating the Bronze Age, and carried on by Viking families. It was also known in Scotland where it appeared in very early days.

The subject having been comprehensively treated, it seemed wise in a second book to dwell more specifically on the subject of designs old and new and to introduce more of the larger specimens of rugs of which photographs had lately been sent to the author. Indeed the field of rug design is so wide that the only limit to illustration is one of expense.

"Rare" hooked rugs are not always of great commercial value. The word is used herein as meaning both very unusual in some cases and valuable in others. Certain rare and certain valuable rugs are equally unfit for practical use on the floor. A fragment of a torn rug may sometimes offer a rare suggestion in design, and also be valuable according to its excellence. Frequently this mere suggestion is of considerable commercial value to the designer, the manufacturer and the dealer. Also collectors are not at all averse to owning even a new rug from such a source and a decorator may and does find it solves his problem perfectly.

This book is an attempt to preserve certain rare hooked designs both old and new for study and criticism, and not alone for mere copying, although that too is of great value for the future of design, when properly followed. Many American firms have reproduced hooked rug patterns excellently in rugs and carpets, as is shown later herein.

It was decided, after study of the best form of presentation, to divide the designs more distinctly into properly titled groups, and where possible give a brief appreciation of each while allowing more space for plates.

To this end several of the leading collectors, importers, makers and dealers were invited to co-operate by sending actual half-tone plates and also photographs.

The response was encouraging and I thank the following firms and individuals who have made full illustration possible:

AIRD & WATSON, New York City
AKAWO CO., A. G. Wirtz, New York City
ANTIQUES MAGAZINE, New York City
ANTIQUARIAN MAGAZINE, New York City
B. ALTMAN & CO., New York City
MRS. P. C. BAUD, St. Catherine's, Ontario, Canada
BIGELOW-SANFORD CO., New York City
L. P. BONFOEY, *President,* Monroe Chemical Co., Quincy, Ill.

[XII]

Mrs. Hazel W. Bullard, Alfred, Me.

Mrs. S. T. Burke, Winnetka, Ill.

Mrs. R. W. Burnham, Ipswich, Mass.

Canadian Rug Importers Co., New York City

R. E. Condon, Upper Darby, Penna.

Flint & Kent, Buffalo, N. Y.

Mrs. A. J. Frazer, El Paso, Texas

John E. Garret, Malden, Mass.

Mrs. C. B. Garretson, Franklin Park, N. J.

Charles Z. Gerhard, Hill, Gerhard Co., New York City

Mrs. Ellen C. Gould, Pasadena, Calif.

Ernest E. Gowell, South Portland, Me.

Mrs. Clair Green, Monmouth Co., N. J.

The Handicrafter Magazine, Jamaica Plain, Mass.

Hardwick & Magee Co., Pennsylvania and New York City

The House Beautiful Magazine, Boston, Mass.

Mrs. F. H. Ingalls, Nashua, N. H.

Mrs. Harry King, Beebe, Ark.

Lord & Taylor, New York City, and Mr. Lebo and Mr. Howe

G. E. Mallinson Importing Co., New York City

Robert F. Martin, Akron, Ohio

Mrs. Pearl K. McGown, West Boylston, Mass.

Mrs. R. E. McRoberts, Lancaster, Ky.

Mr. and Mrs. John B. Moffat, Yonkers, N. Y.

Mohawk Carpet Mills, New York City

Mrs. Lillian Mills Mosseller, New York City

Mrs. Katheryn W. ("Kappy") Neal, Little Rock, Ark.

New England Sales Co., Boston, Mass.

Mrs. A. L. Norton, Boston and Annisquam, Mass.

A. P. Porter, Glen Head, Long Island, N. Y.

Mrs. Reuben Reed, Harvard, Mass.

A. B. Root, Boston, Mass.

The Rural New Yorker, New York City

Mrs. A. J. Saunders, Clinton, Mass.
Mrs. Walter Seabrook, Columbus, Ohio
Mrs. John R. Seth, South Bend, Texas
Mr. J. M. Shoemaker, New York City
Miss Marie Stoker, Lawton, Mich.
Mrs. W. B. Stratton, Montpelier, Vt.
Sure Brothers, New York City and Halifax, N. S.
Mrs. Molly Nye Tobey, Barrington, R. I.
The Villager Magazine, Bronxville, N. Y.
V'Soske Shops, New York City
and very many others.

Of the constant interest of the publishers and staff, and of Mr. Pond personally, in the difficult making of this book, I wish to acknowledge my deep appreciation.

WM. WINTHROP KENT

Orleans, Cape Cod, Mass., September 20, 1941

CONTENTS

[xv]

I

PRIMITIVE

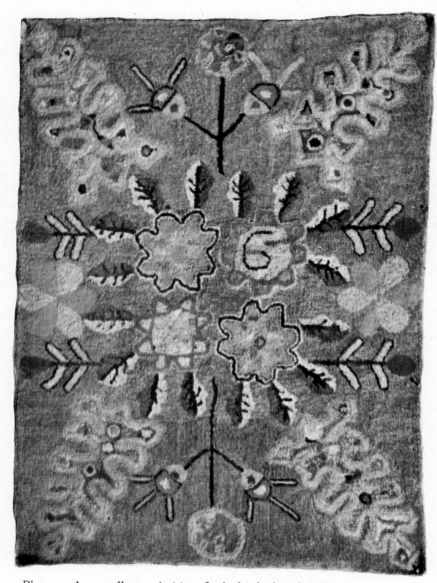

Plate 3. An excellent primitive, finely hooked and well conventionalized.
Found near Philadelphia. Origin unknown.
Size 28″ x 38″

PRIMITIVE

F ONE wishes to learn how far the hooked rug has influenced the designing of both rugs and carpets in America, it is only necessary to talk with some of our most progressive manufacturers, the trend today being *very distinctly toward hooked rug motifs* in both composition and color. Examination of the detail of the latest carpets shows surprisingly often that floral forms and geometrical composition and coloring are closely following not only the highest types of European and American hooking but also that the *primitive* conceptions of obscure farm and village workers are now coming into their own as never before.

Let us hope that the bizarre designs, the purely "crazy quilt" patterns, will not be done to excess. There are, to be sure, strange and queer compositions among them akin to modern or futurist handling which are not only interesting but of great merit and valuable as showing the way to a new development of the craft, while others are so bad as to excite the derision of both the lay public and even of broad-minded designers and critics. Not that public taste is usually correct, for it is often led astray by novelties or impressions made by flashiness and mere queerness, but in the long run we must consider both our public and the decisions of those designers who have justly been ranked high.

Bad designs are now so frequently before us in salesrooms and the numerous private collections of eager amateurs that it is not

W. W. Kent in *The Handicrafter* (Courtesy of publishers)

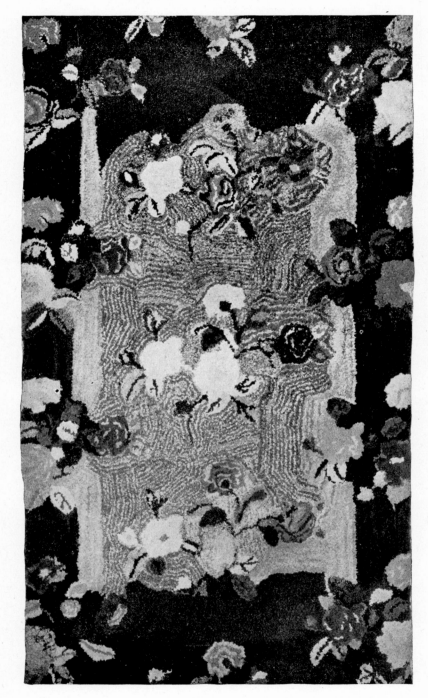

Plate 4. Primitive rug of interesting and somewhat unusual design.

necessary to give examples of them in illustrating this writing, but I hope in showing a few purely primitive plates of the better sort that it can be proved that we are indebted sometimes to unknown farm and village workers for ideas which have in them the germ of very high accomplishment, of very good and sometimes superlative rug and carpet design.

Plate 5. A naïve but perfectly balanced composition both in color and design. Outlined in old rose; otherwise a very delicate combination of grays. 3′ 7″ x 3′ 2″

Why this is so, why we can often, from a crude handling of an original design, work upward from it to a high plane, must be because the original obscure workers, even if ignorant and untaught, felt a breath, perhaps a little temporary breeze, of

[5]

inspiration from their surroundings or conditions of life. It may have, indeed frequently did, come from an almost desperate wish to escape the banality of house or farm work by some heretofore

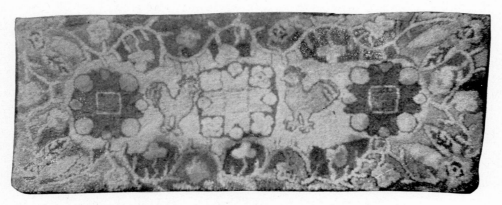

Plate 6. Very effective Early American rug of the farm type.
Collection of Mrs. E. O. Schernikow, New York City.

untried means, to do something which was so engrossing as to steep the mind in an almost oriental dream of the unusual or romantic. All men seek the spice of variety in many ways, and perhaps too often will resort to the stimulant easiest to obtain. But while liquor, coffee, tea, etc., have indeed made us their debtors for brief and productive stimulation, the rug worker often got from the flower garden, the landscape or his own dwelling, something which moderns can only obtain from the same sources or from studying this expression of the early work as to what he saw and so roughly noted.

We must therefore look at crude early rug designs carefully and fairly, and in a sympathetic attitude, to decide whether there is in any one the elusive motive or idea which turned the growing rug into a magic carpet for its maker, on which he or she floated safely away from feeding the pigs, washing dishes, dusting, or even from the poetry of milking time.

I saw, long years ago in a Boston shop, designs both primitive and sophisticated. There was a charm about them all, just as many children are charming even with somewhat dirty faces when they laugh at you over slices of bread and butter and molasses. Children are attractive even when a little mussed and dirty, and so are many hooked rugs, especially the ones from Maine farms. Some in that shop came from Waldoboro, perhaps, and many in

COURTESY AMERICAN ART ASSOCIATION AND OF ARTS MAGAZINE OF FEBRUARY, 1925

Plate 7. Rare Early American rug on heavy homespun linen mesh. Center has ivory field and archaic flowers and fruit with shield above. Gray-black border dotted with red and white flower spray. All materials homespun. Collection of Miss Traver.

[7]

fact from Orono. In Waldoboro beautiful ones seem almost to have grown on bushes ready to be picked by some wise dealer, like Burnham of Ipswich, Creamer of Waldoboro, Yacobian

Plate 8. Farm animals. Not unlike bas-reliefs on stones of underground temple uncovered at Malta a quarter century ago. Collection of Mrs. Lathrop Brown.

Brothers of Boston, or Sure Brothers of New York. Some may have come from New Hampshire before they were caught up by the crowds of collectors who in these latter days appreciated the beauty, saw the intrinsic worth and the charm and value of the craft that had produced them. From Nova Scotian Acadia per-

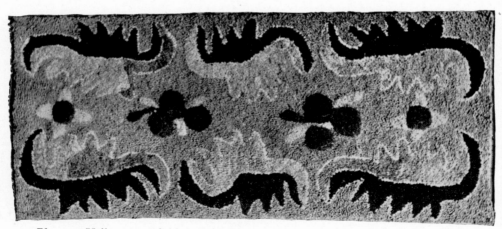

Plate 9. Yellow-gray field with black and pink scrolls and red flowers. Interesting brilliancy and modeling of raised flowers. Made by Mrs. E. Gatchell, Vanceboro, Maine.

haps one or two had floated in. If so, they were the best of all, we know now. I can't recall all the designs of strange flowers that never grew anywhere short of Mars, but they fascinated me. In them were fine color blending, good composition and strange and interesting technique besides the evidence of their earnest creation by fond and careful, though untrained, craftspeople, men and women shut off from cities in the deep snows of northern

Plate 10. Pink flowers with green leaves and brown stems on a dark brown and blue field. Real feeling is shown in composition.

winters who wrought as well and patiently and enthusiastically as they could. Some were very beautiful, some horribly homely no doubt, although I've forgotten any of that sort. All were sincere, of the soil, as well as often soiled, just as they came from floors and hard usage in many homes. They were the output of people who could not loaf long, who must keep hands and mind alert to combat the wear and tear of the daily fight for bread. One wished he could

Plate 11. A rug beautiful in color and of interest to designers because of its architectural character. Size 2' 2" x 5'. From the collection of Mr. John S. Burk, vice-president of B. Altman & Co.

see these people, talk with them, tell them their work was good, that there was in it more than bread and butter to be gained, that many other people of the cities who would see these rugs could sympathize with those who made them, could tell them of their own ancestors who came from similar farms in New and Old England, Scotland, Ireland and Scandinavia. These workers

COURTESY OF PRIVATE COLLECTOR

Plate 12. Rug of clipped wool and probably of Scotch workmanship.
Colors, source and owner unknown.

had indeed made magic carpets, for they swiftly bore my mind searching away, as in the Eastern story, and backward to the scenes of my boyhood in Maine. Although I never had knowingly seen a hooked rug before, nor strangely enough ever heard my New England parents in Bangor speak of this art of which they indeed must have known, I seemed to find them familiar.

Since the question of the origin of hooking was raised by me and discussed in detail in my book, *The Hooked Rug,* an interesting

Plate 13. Illustration showing texture of an unclipped ("mosaic") rug.

research has begun in America and England and probably in Germany. Professor Rudolf Riefstahl of New York, the well-known authority on oriental rugs and other early crafts and activities, told me that he was inclined to favor my supposition that Coptic wool mats or fabrics of a shaggy sort were done by hooking and not pulled tight by needle work over a stick or rod as many people averred. This, if so, and as my book suggests, makes our study of Primitives in rugs even more engrossing and valuable for the craft.

Plate 14. Farm primitive. Field rich blue, brown and black; corner scrolls pinkish red; unknown flower red with green leaves.

FROM A SMALL NEGATIVE BY G. G. DEXTER AND ENLARGED BY CHARLOTTE A. KENT, NEW YORK

Plate 15. A fine primitive from the collection of the late Mr. Arthur Dow of Ipswich, Massachusetts, and made by his grandmother.

Plate 16. Hooked rug (Canadian made) with black and white and blue-gray varied field. Scrolls, white with brown borderlines and very faint pink in some places. Vine leaves, pale green with light brown stems. Center flower, white with red line pattern and orange center. Other flowers white with faint tints of pink, green, etc.; end flowers, varied white and tan with pale blue and white lines. Rare motif. Size 39″ x 71″.

Plate 17. Rugs from New Brunswick and Eastern Maine.

Plate 18. A patriotic rug, American, circa 1820. Heavy, loose hooking. Displays United States flag with sixteen stars, and on outer field original thirteen stars. Size 3′ 6″ x 2′ 7″

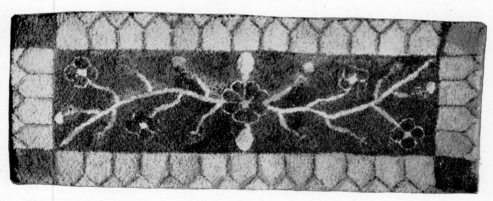

Plate 19. Bedside rug, 24 x 54 inches. Brown flowers with blue stems and buds on speckled black field; varied border in black outlined lozenges of blue, yellow, brown, gray, etc.

[17]

PHOTO BY GENERAL PHOTOGRAPH COMPANY, NEW YORK

Plate 20. A rug in chenille or caterpillar braid, by Miss Mabel Choate.

Plate 21. Group of Maine and Canadian primitives. Center rug, ivory white field, flat red roses, brown basket of flowers and leaves—nondescript forms all. From Mrs. Landers, Topsfield, Maine. She was then 92 years old, of noble French-Canadian blood — a remarkable character. The queer Horn of Plenty rug has a dull light green field, horns dull gray-blue, border line same, and red buds and flowers.

Plate 22. A primitive design, but well balanced and decidedly decorative, perhaps from its direct simplicity. See *Collecting Hooked Rugs* by Elizabeth Waugh and Edith Foley (Century Co., 1917) for the coloring of this design.

Plates 23, 24. Two farm rugs, origin unknown.

PHOTO BY CHARLOTTE AUSTIN KENT, NEW YORK, FROM A SMALL NEGATIVE BY G. G. DEXTER

Plate 25. Old hooked rug, burned with the studio of the late Mr. Arthur Dow, artist, in Ipswich, Massachusetts. The rug was made by his grandmother.

COURTESY R. F. MARTIN, AKRON, OHIO   PHOTO BY CHARLOTTE A. KENT, FROM SMALL NEGATIVE BY G. G. DEXTER

Plate 26. An interesting old rug from the collection of the late Mr. Arthur Dow of Ipswich, Massachusetts. Rug was burned with his studio.

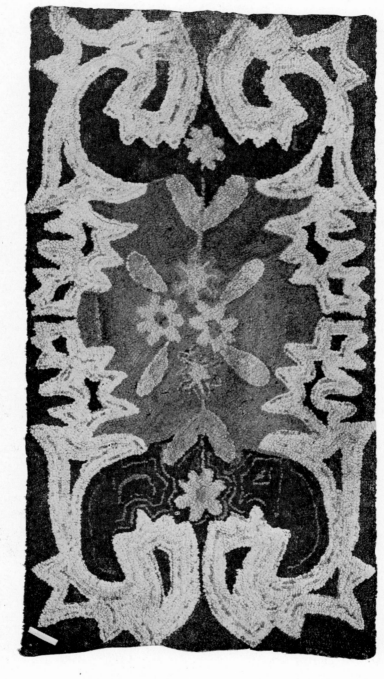

Plate 27. A Labrador rug. All these Labrador rugs are vigorous and suggestive.

II

FLORAL

NATURAL AND CONVENTIONAL

Plate 28. Hooked rug made by Lucy Baker in 1822.

FLORAL

NATURAL AND CONVENTIONAL

LORAL rugs are of two kinds, purely floral and conventional. In some specimens the two are mingled. French and British immigrants — Scotch, English, Irish, Welsh and others — were lovers of flowers, hence found in them many beautiful motifs and inspirations. Their gardens, or even modest window boxes and flower stands, were often the homely sources. To these facts we owe many delightful designs, especially from the French of Acadia and Nova Scotia. Maine and New Hampshire also produced admirable designs and as good work technically. Indeed, the Waldoboro, Maine, and the Durham, New Hampshire, hooked rugs, and some from other towns in New England, are excellently hooked. Some of the sheared or clipped specimens rival the productions of the best French and English looms.

In many New England rugs flowers are so thickly placed as to recall the painted, flower-crowded bowls and boxes of India, as if the worker could not put in too many to recall the masses of bloom in many a garden.

One often sees in hooked rugs modeled flowers, i. e., raised or "hove up," as workers say, above the background or field to emphasize their beauty. These are not always pleasant to walk on, but certainly show the eager ambition of the hooker, and are

[27]

usually good in composition and color. Many of these rugs, some of which come from Northern New England and the Provinces, are worthy to hang in museums and are much prized by collectors. The supply, however, is fast giving out.

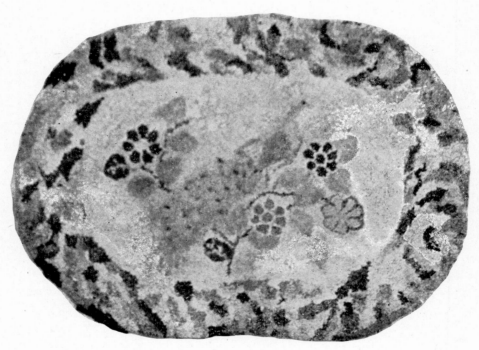

Plate 29. An interesting rug from the collection of the late Mrs. C. L. Norton, of Boston and Annisquam, Mass.

Plate 30. New England hooked rug, made in New Hampshire (circa 1840). Very closely hooked with very small loops. Ground, the color of old pine wood (soft tans). flowers, old rose, blue and soft green — pastel colors. Vegetable-dyed. Size 6′ 7″ x 9′.

Plate 31.

EFORE Their Majesties the King and Queen of Great Britain came to Canada and the United States, Lady Tweedsmuir, at the yearly Toronto Exhibition, selected the hooked rug shown above to be placed in Her Majesty's bedroom at Rideau Hall, Ottawa. This was a well-deserved recognition of the re-invigorated Canadian production of hand-hooked rugs, particularly as carried on in Chetticamp, Cape Breton, where this rug was made.

It is fairly well known that very many of the best rugs were long ago made by the French of Acadia, but after these people were dispersed in Cape Cod and Louisiana (where they are still called "Cageons" or "Caygeons") the art gradually lost excellence and attraction. I believe that immigrants from Scandinavia or Britain brought rug hooking to the Acadians. This is apparent since I found no trace of rug hooking in France, although Mr. Harold Sure of Halifax and New York told me that Father Le Blanc, a Canadian-French priest, assured him that descendants of Acadians in France now carried on the art, but just where he could not state.

When Mrs. Alexander Graham Bell came to Baddeck, Nova Scotia, she was impressed by the possibilities and domestic value of hooking as a

n's Rug.

home industry. Miss M. Lillian Burke of New York, at Mrs. Bell's instiga-
tion, began the improvement of this and other handicrafts in Nova Scotia.
At Chetticamp, Cape Breton, as Miss Burke discovered, is a district inhab-
ited by descendants of early French settlers. Here, also, besides the rug for
the Queen's room, was made in 1938 the largest hooked rug of which I
have note, 18 x 36 feet (see page 77). It was the work of more than eight
women who finished it in six months. Many rugs are made here on orders
from "the States." At Chetticamp there are also excellent hookers among
the men. To Miss Burke, who insists on exact methods in design, color
dyeing, and general technique, has come great praise and success.

More explicit descriptions of all the Chetticamp products were carefully written in 1939 by Mrs. Corolyn Cox for the Montreal *Standard,
The Christian Science Monitor,* and other periodicals.

One other large rug, 18 x 28 feet, was made a few years ago at the late
Mr. R. W. Burnham's studio, Ipswich, Massachusetts, for a New York
home, and another, size unknown, in black basket-pattern surrounding small
red squares, by the Hearthstone Studios of Miss A. M. Laisé Phillips, New
York City.

[31]

PHOTO BY MATTIE EDWARDS HEWITT

Plate 32. Border too emphatic in tone.

COURTESY OF TOWN AND COUNTRY MAGAZINE

Plate 33. Early American hooked carpet — tortoise-shell brown field, with small rosetted crimson and pink central medallion and arched lobed borders enriched with sprays of similarly colored flowers. Size 8' 9" x 8' 9".

Plate 34. Rich floral composition. The stars give a sparkle to the dark band
which may symbolize the sky at night.

Plate 35. "Ring-Around-Rosy." Adapted from two designs in Metropolitan Museum. Drawn and hooked by Mrs. Harry King of Batesville, Arkansas.

Plate 36. "Colonial Bouquet." Designed by Mrs. Harry King and worked by Mrs. Kenneth Riddle of Little Rock, Arkansas.

COLOR PLATES COURTESY OF PUTNAM FADELESS DYES, MANUFACTURED BY
MONROE CHEMICAL COMPANY, QUINCY, ILLINOIS,
THE DYES USED BY MRS. KING

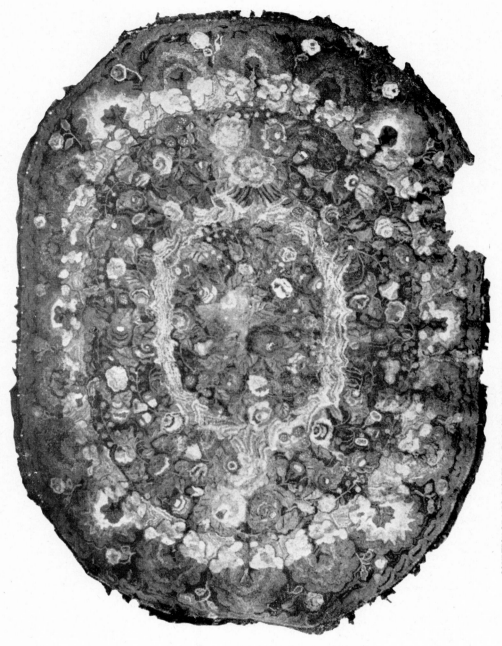

Plate 37. Hooked rug, made by Harriet Emery, of Alfred, Maine. Sold at a Portland auction, as shown, for $2055, repaired at an expense of $500, and sold to a prominent New York firm for $4500. They sold it to the governor of a southern state. Size, 10' x 12'. (From this Mrs. Caroline Saunders, Clinton, Mass., and Mrs. Hazel W. Bullard, Alfred, Maine, each made a reproduction.)

Plate 38. Rug excellently made in China from a design by W. W. Kent.

Plate 39. Origin unknown.

Plates *40, 41.* Two Early American rugs.

[39]

Plate 42. Unusual rococo composition. Designer unknown.

Plate 43. Hooked (or woven) rug of 1802, signed PM.

Plate 44. Hooked rug, made in China from a design by W. W. Kent.

Plates 45, 46. Two New England rugs of note — realistic floral of the Maine type.

[43]

Plate 47. A New Hampshire product. Blue field, shaded darker outwardly from center. Early American, clipped.

Plate 48. Conventional floral in French manner.

[45]

COURTESY OF J. M. SHOEMAKER

Plate 49. Rare floral medallion, hooked carpet, Early American. Fine compact hooking. Gray oval medallion finely scalloped in sapphire-blue; occupied by bouquet of closely placed blue and crimson flowers; golden-tan field scrolled in yellow and red. Large red scrollings and outer black borders having floral and leaf corners. 8′ 9″ x 7′ 5″.

[46]

Plate 50. Two rugs suggestive of needlepoint.

Plate 51. Beautiful massing of both realistic and conventional flowers.

Plates 52, 53. Two Early American rugs.

Plate 54. Early American hooked carpet. Close, fine hooking. Black oblong center occupied by large crimson and blue flowers, surrounded by a field of tan; scrolled with red leaf motifs and outer border of gray. Tortoise shell-black major borders with leaf scrollings in alternate lavender, pinks, yellow and crimson tones. Size, 7′ 7″ x 6′.

Plates 55, 56. Two rugs from the collection of Mrs. R. W. Burnham, upper one a beautiful threshold rug now in a private collection.

COURTESY OF
J. M. SHOEMAKER COMPANY, NEW YORK

Plate 57. Good conventional design in scrolls. Light blue field with red and tan scroll border. Modeled bouquet of lavender and red flowers. 5′ x 2′ 8″. Sold for $140.

Plate 58. From the collection of Mrs. J. K. Brown, Fort Bliss, Texas.

Plate 59. Excellent floral massing.

Plate 60. Large hooked carpet, showing fine and varied treatment of scrolls especially in the rococo border to the excellent floral center.

FROM MR. AND MRS. R. W. BURNHAM'S COLLECTION (NOW DISPERSED)

Plate 61. (Upper)   Tan or cream field, red scroll. Size 2' 9" x 5' 2".
Plate 62. (Center) Gray field, flower natural, not clipped. Size 2' 10" x 6'.
Plate 63. (Lower)   Mottled field, black, tans and browns. Size 3' 1" x 5' 8".

Plate 64. A rare and beautiful design of excellent composition, from the collection of Miss Ethelyn Cobb, Treasure Island Shop, Buffalo, New York.

Plate 65. Natural and conventional floral, showing Nova Scotian influence.

Plate 66. An Early American from Charles Z. Gerhard, New York City.
Size 7′ 8″ x 7′ 9″.

Plate 67. Rug made from Frost Pattern No. 60. (See "A Yankee Rug Designer," p. 173.) Stencils now owned by Mrs. W. B. Stratton, Montpelier, Vermont.

Plate 68. Made in New Durham, N. H., home of famous 19th century hooked rug workers, by one of the best craftsmen. Priced at $2500.

Plate 69. Primitive floral branches in brilliant tones on gray-black. The wide border has rose and gold scrolls, a small dog in each corner, and an edge simulating tasseled fringe. All wool yarn. Excellent design. Size 7′ 5″ x 6′ 6″.

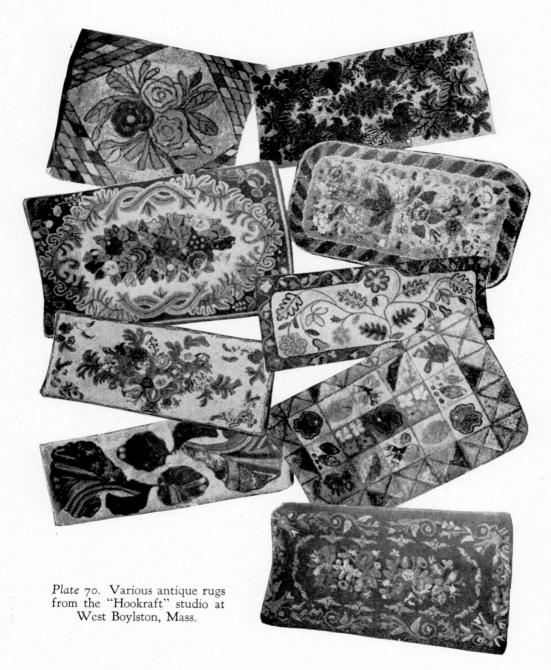

Plate 70. Various antique rugs
from the "Hookraft" studio at
West Boylston, Mass.

Plate 71. Floral wreath medallion hooked carpet, American (circa 1820). Close hooking; rich tan field occupied by an oval bouquet and broad wreath of extremely varied flowers — lilies, roses, Canterbury bells and asters in pastel colors and rose-crimson. Scrolled red and old yellow leaf border following the contour of the wreath and forming large corners. Size 8' 6" x 6' 5".

Plates 72, 73. Two oval-shaped rugs from the collection of Mrs. R. W. Burnham. One at left has red and pink flowers with dark veins against a field of light gray. At right, raised, or modeled, natural flowers on a tan field.

Plate 74. A varied collection of rugs from the workshop of
Mrs. Al J. Frazer, at El Paso, Texas.

Plate 75. Rug, at least seventy years old, made by Sarah H. Roberts, of Wayne, Maine.
Now owned by Mary Swett, Vienna, Maine.

Plate 76. A grand century-old rug, made near Portland, Maine. Property of Ernest E. Gowell of South Portland. Center ground — prevailing color, cream. Center floral medallion and center floral wreath — flowers and leaves in many shades of green, red, crimsons and browns. Flowers tinted with blues, lavender, orchid, orange and yellow. Small scrolls, old flannel red; large scrolls, shades of tan to brown — all outlined and interwoven with black. Ground from small scrolls to border — shaded tans to dark browns. Side border scrolls — blended shades of red and crimson outlined and interwoven with black and cream. Corners — roses, vines and leaves, shades of red, green and brown. Border, aged black. Size 6′ 2″ x 8′ 10″.

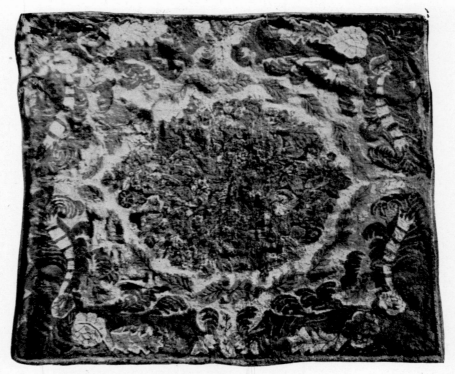

Plate 77. Antique rug, beautiful low tones, tans, blues, grays, pale reds, etc.
Shows slight oriental trend. About 6½′ x 8′.

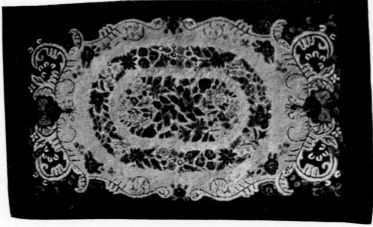

Plate 78. "Anglo-Saxon Wreath," designed by Kappy Neal, Little Rock, Ark.

Plate 79. Magnificent large rug. Tan field, flowers pastel shades of blue and red. Made in Maine about 1875 by a cousin of Mr. R. E. Condon, of Upper Darby, Pa., who now owns it. Size 6′ 1″ x 8′ 6″.

Plate 80. Livingroom of Mrs. Audrey Seabrook of Columbus, Ohio. The rug shown, adapted by her from an old one, is 9′ 6″ x 12′ 3″.

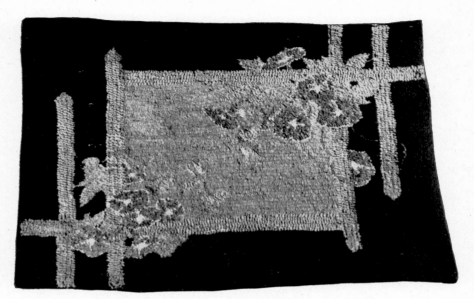

Plate 81. Rug designed by **Mrs. Al J. Frazer** and
Mrs. Lois Denton, El Paso, Texas.

Plate 82. Floral rug with oval wreath of flowers on black, surrounded by garlands.
Border of fine scrolls. Length, 5′ 2″; width, 3′ 5″.

Plate 83. "Hookraft" prize rug, made by Mrs. Reuben Reed of Harvard, Mass.

Plate 84. A memorial rug. The vase under the weeping willow once had initials on it. Collection of the late Mrs. C. L. Norton of Boston and Annisquam, Mass., who was noted for her success in extracting dyes from garden and wild flowers and her deep appreciation of handicraft and the arts, old and new. This rug is *very old,* fine in texture, good coloring and delicate, and is used now as mural decoration on old wooden sheathing.

Plate 85. Companion rug to one shown in plate 11 on page 10. From the collection of John S. Burk, vice-president of B. Altman & Company, New York. Size 2′ 3″ x 5′ 7″.

Plate 86. Three modern rugs made by Mrs. John R. Seth, South Bend, Texas

Upper, "Autumn Leaves." Leaves, shades of brown; flowers, deep red and brick red tones and dull golds; field, olive green with modeled green leaves. Size 2½' x 4½'.

Center, "Betty's Ribbon." Scroll from old rugs. Flowers of lavender and yellow from ribbon worn on Betty's bonnet. Size 2½' x 4½'.

Lower, "Colonial Rose." Old pattern, new coloring. Roses, two shades of red; leaves, green; stripes, reds, browns, greens, yellows, etc. Size 3' x 6'.

Plate 87. Two rugs of the Aubusson style. Upper one from W. & J. Sloane. Lower one from F. Schumacher and Company.

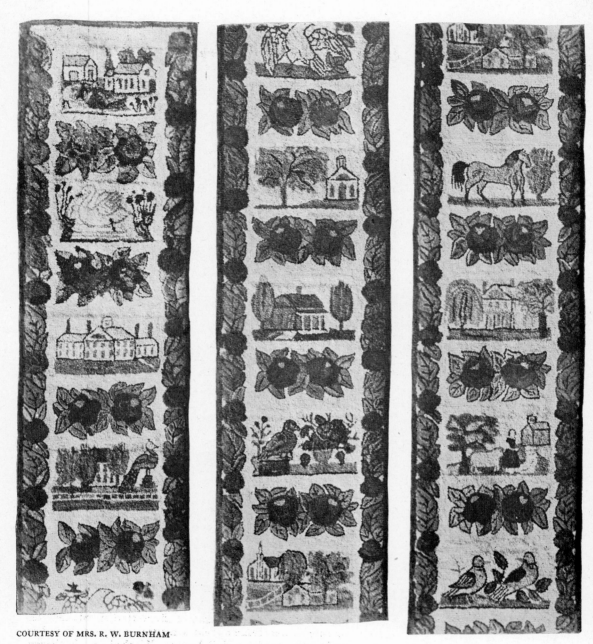

Plate 88. Stair carpet. Every riser has its own design.

Plate 89. Floral hooked carpet. Mass of flowers in shades of rose, maroon, lavender and mauve on light ground. Border of blue interlacing bands and floral corners. Sheared woolen material. Size 10′ x 9′.

Plate 90. The first rug designed and hooked sixty years ago by Miss Minnie Light of Burkettsville, Maine. Exquisite flower designs, field a neutral gray, scrolls a deep red, outer border a dull brown. Worked on old, heavy, white cotton cloth. Size 27″ x 54″.

Plate 91. This magnificent rug, 18′ x 36′, probably the largest hand-hooked rug in existence, was an adaptation by Persian Rug Manufactory of a Savonerie rug design in the Louvre. The rug was drawn by Miss M. Lillian Burke and hooked under her direction by eight of her Cheticamp (Cape Breton) workers, six months being required for completion of the work.

Plate 92. This large rug, 16′ x 21′, was designed by Miss M. Lillian Burke and hooked by seven of her Cheticamp (Cape Breton) workers. The design is white magnolias on a soft green background.

Plate 93. From the collection of Mrs. J. K. Brown, Fort Bliss, El Paso, Texas.

Plates 94, 95. Two modern rugs, one above hooked by G. E. T. Ward, D. D., Orleans, Massachusetts, the other by Mrs. Ward.

Plate 96. From Frost pattern No. 10. Dark gray field, flowers natural, soft blue tone. Size 2′ 6″ x 4′ 2″.

Plate 97. Rug made by Mary C. Barstow over fifty years ago from design by an art teacher. Photo contributed by Miss Marie Stoker, Lawton, Michigan.

Plate 98. "Carolina Rose," a design of morning glories and roses. By Kappy Neal, of Little Rock, Arkansas.

Plate 99. "French Bouquet," an all floral design also by Kappy Neal. Drawn from fresh garden flowers.

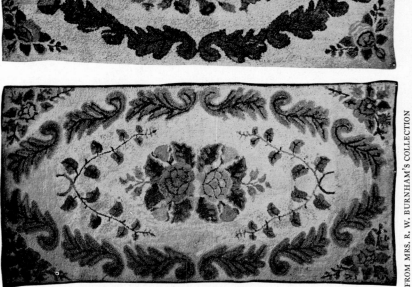

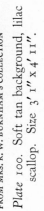

FROM MRS. R. W. BURNHAM'S COLLECTION

Plate 100. Soft tan background, lilac scallop. Size 3′ 1″ x 4′ 11″.

Plate 101. Soft tan-coffee background. Natural flowers. Soft green wreath of leaves. Size 3′ 3″ x 5′ 6″.

Plate 102. White field, soft flowers; leaves, gray, blue, soft browns, etc. Size 3′ x 5′ 7″.

The late R. W. Burnham Collection was one of the finest in the United States. Both he and Mrs. Burnham have been of great assistance in the compilation of this book and "The Hooked Rug."

Plate 103. An unusual hooked pattern — probably part of a larger rug. Freely floral and quite delicately treated.

Plate 104. A "Hookraft" rug from West Boylston, Mass.

[83]

Plates 105 · 110. These chair mats from Mrs. C. V. Miller, Bowling Green, Kentucky, remind us of the adaptability of the art of hooking to other uses than floor covering.

Plate 111. This attractive old-fashioned bouquet, 57" x 32", is composed of an interesting aggregation of flowers on a field of ivory. Roses, lilies, tulips, morning glories, pansies and other blooms blend together within a border of black scroll work and still more flowers. The handiwork of Mrs. C. V. Miller of Bowling Green, Kentucky.

Plate 112. Rug made by Mrs. Hazel W. Bullard, Alfred, Maine. An adaptation of old floral designs used by Minnie Light fifty or sixty years ago.

Plate 113. Modern rug made by Mrs. F. H. Ingalls of Nashua, N. H.

Plate 114. Canadian rug of pastel tints. Red roses and pale leaves
on superb hit-or-miss field of brown, black and gray stripes.
Size about 4' 6" x 8'.

Plate 115. From the Caswell Barrie Collection. Probably Acadian - French from Nova Scotia. Mr. Barrie's collection, now dispersed, was a notable one indeed. **(See also "The Hooked Rug" for other plates he kindly contributed.)**

Plate 116. An interesting grape design from the collection of Mrs. R. W. Burnham.

Plate 117. Reproduction by Mrs. Hazel W. Bullard of an old rug made fifty years ago by her mother, Clara Wigfall Wallace. Locked leaf and strawberry pattern.

III

FLORAL GEOMETRICAL

Plate 118. "Star of Bethlehem," conventional scrolls and realistic flowers.

FLORAL GEOMETRICAL

F ALL the designs for hooked rugs the floral geo-metrical is the most interesting and usually the best artistically. It is not difficult for anyone to design a purely floral composition, but to arrange flowers and geometric lines and spaces in beautiful and harmonious order requires talent of no mean order.

Yet we find this often done in hooked rugs by people who, in the evident absence of special training, must have possessed inher-ent talent with considerable inspiration.

It takes a master to conventionalize flowers so as to escape the commonplace. Many workers in town or farm not being designers found long ago that natural flower forms could be made acceptably artistic in rugs by combining them in composition with geometric forms.

Oriental rug designers knew this art well, but after long years of designing direct, conventionalizing became to them even easier than using the natural forms, which often themselves became geometric and finally lost floral characteristics in meaningless pat-terns, though sometimes producing remarkably decorative forms, lines and medallions as we see in the beautiful Mina Khani rugs.

The floral geometrical field offers the greatest chances for beau-tiful design in endless permutations and combinations. Flowers sinuously offset the rigidity of lines and angles, triangles, squares, pentagons, hexagons, etc. Stepped medallions, diamonds, ovals, all invite the addition of flowers, natural and conventional. Rug

merchants tell me that floral geometric rugs are the most popular with their customers and that those in which tans and taupe
tones occupy the field are in the long run the most commercially
successful. Rose pinks are also sought for in backgrounds and

Plate 119. "Cousin Julia" is another product of Mrs. C. V. Miller of
Bowling Green, Kentucky. Roses, morning glories, lilies, etc., comprise the
center display against a field of browns and tan. The border line and lattice-
like corners are a blending of red and black on a background of cool taupe.
Size 53″ x 29″.

sometimes a restrained use of black enriches the patterns as
nothing else can.

Of late years a mingling of free leaf forms, fern-like branches,
emphasized with geometrically new, queer medallions or insets,
are considerably in vogue, all tending to return to styles which the
Koreans and especially the Chinese and later the Japanese designers affected.

[92]

When I am asked what I think of the so-called "modernism" of today with its merely queer and often ugly, lifeless characters, I am reminded of a story told by John B. Moffat of a darkey who, when asked what he thought of the coinage of silver 16 to 1, replied, "Wal, I'll tell you what I think; I jus' *don't* think!" Moffat, schooled for years in the best traditions of design, could appreciate this as applied to much "modernism" and yet admire the best compositions of modern designers, especially where they made rare hits in what are known as "textiles" — designs revealing more or less the materials of the fabric and method of production.

Plate 120. "The Arkansas," designed and made by Mrs. Harry King, Batesville, Arkansas. Contains the rose, pansy, cotton bolls and leaves, the strawberry and a rice field when the rice is "in the boot."

Plate 121. A Labrador rug of attractive design.

One of the strongest claims to excellence which the hooked rug advances is its revelation of the aforementioned characteristics. Indeed, no oriental rug can imitate honestly the mosaic character of an unclipped hooked rug, while clipped ones appeal to the best Chinese designers, who follow the antique school judiciously.

Geometrical forms are often used successfully in combination with medallions of abstract design not even based on floral suggestion.

Plate 122. Nova Scotian clipped-wool hooked rug. One of the best combinations of numerous colors on a tan field that I can recall. Origin unknown. Carefully hooked and clipped. Size roughly 5′ x 8′.

Plate 123. Part of a very early runner, found in Guilford, Conn., by Dorothy Glen, who has an antique shop in that town.

PHOTO BY CLYDE C. BROWN, FRANKLIN, N. H.

Plate 124. From the collection of Mrs. J. K. Brown, Fort Bliss, Texas.

Plate 125. This design was made for a room-size rug. Very soft autumn shades of beige and browns. Made in Homecraft Studio by Mrs. Ellen C. Gould of Pasadena, California.

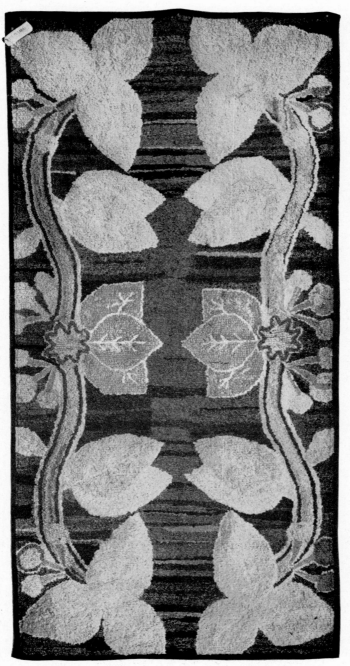

Plate 126. A characteristic Labrador rug.

Plate 127. A Labrador rug of considerable interest.

Plate 128. A well-designed all-over geometrical and floral.
Now in a private collection.

Plate 129. New England rug found in Nova Scotia.
Homespun material. Size 3′ x 6′.

Plate 130. Rug at top shows old-fashioned rose design, from George E. Mallinson. Lower, grape (?) design, from Canadian Hooked Rug Importers.

Plates 131, 132. Canadian rugs about three feet square. Interest lies in the emphasis of outline. From the Sure Collection, now dispersed.

Plate 133. Rug with unusual border. From a private collection.

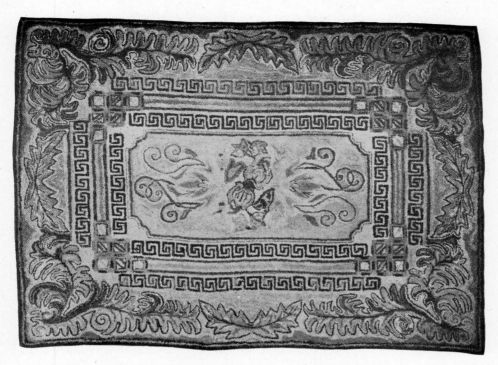

Plate 134. Interesting contrast of conventional scrolls with the Roman key, which would be used only as a border in an Oriental rug. From a private collection.

IV

GEOMETRICAL

Plate 135. A Labrador rug of the geometrical type.

GEOMETRICAL

THE geometrical designs in hooked rugs reveal knowl-
edge of an unusual sort, not in the forms of the
single patterns but chiefly where the designer has
mingled and often interlaced several geometric forms
to agreeably deceive the eye. Perhaps a half dozen
or more mere line patterns are, in some of the finer rugs, used
together, crossing and interlacing.

It is not surprising that Moors, Berbers, Saracens, Arabs and
other earlier races knew the worth of this, but it is noteworthy
that such designs came often from farm and village workers in
America who had traveled and read little or not at all but were
probably keen observers.

In this we must ascribe a considerable influence to the objects
which sailors and officers brought home to friends and relatives
from Africa, Asia, Europe and the South Seas. These articles
were educationally suggestive.

Early and later American workers in textiles, wood and metal,
were fond of geometric designs. Eighteenth century examples of
them are numerous, from the simple star and other forms scratched
or incised on wooden boxes and brass warming pans to the more
ambitious attempts in marquetry, embossed book covers, and
hooked rugs. The latter, if not proving an actual acquaintance
with the beautiful book-cover designs done for Grolier, the French
bibliophile, and the still more elegant and refined designs done in
Persia and Egypt, nevertheless tell us that a similar fondness for

geometric combinations inspired both the early oriental and the late western designers.

It is well known that some of the finest interlaces and geometric patterns in general on Persian rugs were suggested by the borders and centers of Persian book covers, and these in turn were some-

Plate 136. Two early Canadian rugs; wool, unclipped.

times taken from the pages of illuminated manuscripts and surely inspired many designs made for Grolier. American and English book covers of the Victorian period suggest the patterns of hooked rugs.

Certain purely geometrical patterns were noticeably popular with rug makers. In these they found a use for small odds and ends of material especially in such designs as blocks, cubes, stars, rondels, crescents, etc., not to mention the wavy or the marbleized backgrounds.

This use accounts, too, for the preponderance of "hit or miss" work in hooked rugs, where it so often fills geometric spaces effectively.

The beauty of variegated wavy and striped backgrounds in many a New England and Canadian rug rivals the work of Orientals. It is one of the valuable contributions to rug design given by hooked rug workers.

COURTESY OF LORD & TAYLOR   PHOTO BY UNDERWOOD AND UNDERWOOD

Plate 137. A Labrador rug.

Plate 138. A Labrador rug.

Plate 139. A Labrador rug.

Plate 140. Three geometrical rugs; one at left, from the collection of Mrs. H. K. White, Boston, Mass.; one at the right from the collection of Miss C. M. Kent, Buffalo, N. Y.; while the lower one is from Mrs. J. K. Brown's collection, Fort Bliss, Texas.

Plate 141. Early American. An unusual rug of remarkably fine quality. Border, hit-and-miss in many shades, with tessellated corners in graduating colors in grays and reds. Center, a rare design in motley colors of brilliant hue covered with conventional diamond patterns composed of smaller diamonds in graduating colors. Size 8′ 3″ x 6′ 4″.

[113]

Plate 142. Effective variations in patterns and colors of medallions.

Plates 143, 144. Two rugs from the Islands of Sumba or Rotti, Malay Archipelago, Dutch East Indies. Now in Buffalo Museum of Natural History.

V

ANIMAL LIFE

Plate 145. "Lion Rug," made shortly after the Revolutionary War. The British lion forms the centerpiece and American eagles with outspread wings guard the corners. Size 9′ 6″ x 10′.

ANIMAL LIFE

MERICAN hooked rug designs often include the portrayal of animals while oriental rugs, other than Persian, seldom do. This is interesting as revealing that many Orientals and Latins have not the love for animals that Western people generally have, many of the older civilizations not showing great attachment to or even consideration for the lower forms of life. The camel driver, I noted once at Tozeur, Africa, will feed his camel date stones to ease the pains of hunger, thinking possibly that he is promoting digestion. The donkey boy in Italy and in Egypt will cruelly overload his donkey, and dogs in the East are usually considered pests, not pets, and treated accordingly. The great exception to this is the love of the Arab for his horse, or his falcon, although he is not always considerate of them.

Dogs, horses, cats, rabbits, birds, and also deer, lions and wild animals generally are shown on American hooked rugs. Domestic pets are frequently drawn and colored with loving care and sometimes well executed anatomically in lifelike action. The farmer of the temperate zone passes much of his life with animals. He loves his dog, the housewife her cat. Rabbits and chickens find their ways to the brief immortality of the floor rug or bedspread, often with names, dates and mottoes or legends. Especially is this true of the designs of English-speaking people and Nordics in general, for they cherish the recollection of cold weather companionship passed with pets during many wintry hours.

So we can usually trace the origin of an "animal rug" to a Nordic source and be pretty sure it was not made by a person of Latin or Oriental blood, although there are notable exceptions to the rule.

The dog and cat are the favorite subjects for hooking in the animal class of design, but horses run them a close second and sometimes are capitally drawn — as in plates No. 153 and 161.

This constant exhibition of human love for animals, rivaling that for flowers and ornament, is a humanizing influence which man needs today more than ever before. To care for many things besides self is what solitude often demands. It is a wholesome

Plate 146. Spirited primitive rug.

outlet for human emotions, lacking which relief one's health may become jeopardized. That isolated human beings know this, is constantly proven by their rug designs, especially those of animals.

COLLECTION OF MRS. J. K. BROWN

Plate 147. White rabbit on blue, black and brown field; red corner sprays and white, red, blue and gray cartouche.

In the stamped or stenciled patterns sold in many places in the latter part of the nineteenth century the animals were usually crudely drawn, at least in the catalogs thereof. This may possibly account for many of the anatomical errors in the finished rugs, but I believe there has been an improvement made in this direction, especially by the designs issued by the late R. W. Burnham, Ipswich, Massachusetts, and certain Vermont and Maine dealers in patterns. E. S. Frost & Company, Biddeford, Maine, issued a pattern book in bright crude colors. This was much used in Maine. (See Chapter X.)

Plate 148. Appears to be a tiger enjoying the comforts of a hooked rug.

Plate 149. An idealized portrait of a Welsh setter that belonged to Horace Kent Tenney. Colors are blues, greens and pale yellow; gray dog. Signed and dated 1925.

COLLECTION OF MRS. J. K. BROWN

Plate 150

[123]

Plate 151. Animal rug from the Mrs. R. W. Burnham Collection.

Plate 152. Oval medallion, with figure of a tan and ivory spaniel seated on a red, black and gray tile floor. Finished with leaf scrollings and black border having crimson corners. Early American, Frost pattern. Size 3′ 7″ x 2′ 9″.

[124]

Plate 153. Far-Canadian farm animal rugs. Excellent draughtsmanship in all of these. Three lower ones from the collection of Mrs. John K. Brown.

Plate 154. Silvery ivory field, cat and kittens seated on red rug. Crimson and green floral corners. Early American, Frost pattern No. 39. 4′ 3″ x 2′ 7″.

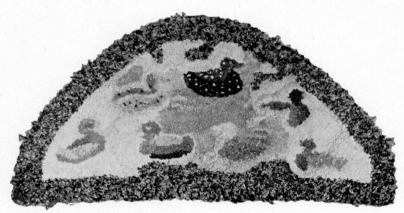

Plate 155. A threshold rug.

Plate 156. Early American. Fluctuating black field. Size 4′ 4″ x 2′ 6″.

Plate 157. Early American. Ivory field, water fowl standing amid crimson and blue flowers. Crimson and tawny black borders. Size 3′ 3″ x 1′ 5″.

[127]

Plate 158. Primitive from Northern Ohio. Lion and Palms design from E. Ross & Co.'s book No. 7. Often used, origin unknown. Also used by E. S. Frost. (See Chapter X)

Plate 159

Plate 160. A fine old needlepoint rug, about 125 years old.

Plate 161. Early American animal rug with fluctuating gray field; chestnut horse standing before well-head; a potted flower at right. Crimson border. Size 4′ 3″ x 2′ 2″.

Plate 162. Large patriotic rug. Diagonal band in red, white and blue. Made in East Liberty, Maine, in early XIX century. For many years hung in a Maine tavern, later possibly in the State House, Augusta, Maine. Size 14′ x 10′.

VI
STILL LIFE

Plate 163. Basket of flowers, very decorative, wide border, although primitive.

STILL LIFE

ACK of skill in draughtsmanship and the inability to procure prints of animals or flowers for copying possibly led to the representation in rugs of everyday implements, utensils and furniture. The kitchen clock, a pump, a jug or pitcher, basket or flower pot are commonly used, and the trellis, the fireplace, and even the sticks from the woodpile, are often introduced in patterns in Canadian rugs along with maple leaves. The entire house and barn with paths and fences were and still are wrought in farm

COURTESY OF MRS. R. W. BURNHAM

Plate 164. Bird and nest pattern. Center field cream, outer field olive.
Size 2′ 4″ x 3′ 1″.

[133]

Plate 165. Basket and fruit. Awarded first prize at a fair in 1838 by the
Maine Charitable Mechanic Association.

Plate 166. Louis XVI Savonnerie rug. Beautiful composition, strangely
like the best type of Acadian hooked rugs from Nova Scotia. Inspiring
to hooked rug designers, with its vase and horns of plenty.

rugs, often better in drawing and coloring than the crude pictures painted on glass for clocks and mirror tops. These are found in so-called primitives.

Perhaps the basket filled with flowers has always had the strongest appeal for rug makers in rural districts, but many are the strange horns-of-plenty shown and often reversed toward each other for balance in design.

Plate 167. Jardiniere rug (American 18th century). Interesting golden-yellow field, displaying a deeper-toned jardiniere filled with quaintly-drawn crimson, pink and lavender flowers with similar flower sprays at corners. Size 3′ 9″ square.

[135]

Plate 168. Floral basket. Black mottled field, tans and browns.
Size 2′ 4″ x 3′ 6″.

VII

NAUTICAL

ILLUSTRATED IN THE ARTS MAGAZINE, FEBRUARY, 1925

Plate 169. Important Early American rug, about 1820, fashioned upon a ground of homespun linen in colored wools by a method known as *reedstitch.* Silhouette of the packet ship "John Talpey" flying the Black Ball Line pennant, on azure blue ground. On the left is presumably the fort at Governor's Island flying the American flag; at right, a lighthouse also flying the American flag. In the upper center and either corner, a five-pointed star, and below, on an olive-green ground, the name of the ship. Narrow mauve border with olive-green corners; lovely composition of color. The Black Ball Line was established in 1816 as a line of packets between New York and Liverpool by some far-sighted Quaker capitalists, and sailed the first of every month. It was famous for the brutality of its officers and was probably the cause of the well-known chanty —

> In the Black Ball Line I served my time,
> Hurrah for the Black Ball Line!

NAUTICAL

LONG the northeastern seacoast of North America boats, ships, anchors and other motifs from sea life have produced both crude and excellent rug designs, sometimes done by wife or sweetheart and often by sailors themselves. Hooking is an ancient craft aboard ship, first done to prevent chafing of ropes in the rigging and later for decorative purposes at home.* Many retired seamen can and do make rugs ashore today, and I feel sure that the men taught the craft to the women, even in the Bronze Age when Viking ships raided southern lands and brought back loot which may, too, have suggested patterns.

So the examples of rugs with ships of all kinds pictured on them are numerous, often with the name of the vessel or some motto or legend like "Outward Bound" or "Homeward Bound" and possibly a date. As far as I know such rugs are usually of American make by English-speaking people. No examples made in Scandinavia or Scotland, England or Ireland, have come to my notice, yet very possibly such might be found now by patient searchers. East coast villagers of England I know are hooked rug makers, but the designs are quite crude, with little meaning. They are greatly used by the fisher folk whose men do not take long fishing or trading voyages, as the Americans and the Basques did and do. Why the latter do not hook rugs is a question I cannot answer. There are, it was said by a Canadian priest to a

*See "The Hooked Rug" once more.

friend of mine, hooked rugs made in France by exiled French Acadians, but I have not yet been able to learn where they still carry on the craft they learned in Canada. If it were on the French coast we ought to find ships, etc., on their rugs, together with names and dates.

The chain-like borders on rugs made in Northeastern America are not always ships' chains I have been told, but are meant for cables inspired by the laying of the Atlantic cable by Cyrus Field. Why a chain and not a cable was so used is a mystery. I am inclined to believe that the chain is merely a symbol of friendship, security or good fortune, as such rugs usually have floral decoration and no suggestion of the sea. I recall, however, seeing some rugs that had rope-like cables on them.

Plate 170. An excellently designed nautical rug made by Miss A. L. Tenney of Appleton, Wisconsin.

Plate 171

VIII

LANDSCAPE

Plate 172. Landscape with bird life. Origin unknown.

LANDSCAPE

WHETHER landscape is a proper subject for representation on rugs is an open question. Personally I do not like to walk on a landscape, but why should we walk on rugs showing flowers or fish or ships? Yet we do, and even admire them at the time. Often landscaped rugs were made to hang on the wall of the country parlor or lie in front of the parlor fireplace or airtight stove in that room, which was generally little used. Probably no amount of criticism would have prevented their making and they must have gratified a desire that the maker could not for some reason satisfy with paint and canvas. The makers of one or two rugs I've seen certainly could have creditably rendered their subjects in oil, so good were the composition and color values, perspective and drawing.

But no matter how much such rugs may be valued for their subject and technique when not made for use on the floor, yet far superior for this purpose are geometrical, floral or abstract designs. The mosaic workers in the Baptistry at Ravenna, Italy, executed wall designs that, as art, rival or excel many a landscape painting, although they are only graceful patterns in marvelously blended colors of strong tones with most delicate gradations.

The design, "A Massachusetts Rug" (Plate No. 178), was undoubtedly created by a Maine sea captain who traveled to foreign countries. In all probability he was deeply impressed with the architectural construction of castles and upon his return home

from a sea voyage drew the picture shown on this rug and his wife hooked it. As you will note, in the foreground is a typical New England home. It is constructed on homemade linen canvas, and experts claim that the material used was made on a hand loom and believe the rug to be over 100 years old.

Plate 173. A collection of landscapes from the Provinces by Miss Ursula Toomey of Springfield, Mass.

Miss Toomey has traveled through the Maritime Provinces of Eastern Canada — Nova Scotia, New Brunswick, and Prince Edward Island — collecting interesting examples of this fireside industry. From remote fishing villages on the shores of the Bay of Fundy, from the deep woods of New Brunswick, from the picturesque island of Grand Manan, from the farthermost tip of Prince Edward Island, she has brought colorful rugs reflecting the art, industry and resourcefulness of these isolated folk.

[146]

Plate 174. Three delightful landscape rugs made from drawings by C. B. Garretson, Franklin Park, New Jersey. Top, Washington's birthplace at Bridges Creek, Virginia. Drawn from a small newspaper picture. 48″ x 30″. Center, "Taking the Back Track" (from a Currier & Ives print). This rug won first prize at Eastern States Exposition, Springfield, Mass., where between 500 and 600 rugs were entered. 28″ x 22″. Lower rug, farm scene from a Currier & Ives. 46″ x 28″.

Plate 175. Hooked rug (before 1835). Worked by Emily Trask Barnard and depicting her home at Dixfield Common, Maine, with her horse Betsy in the foreground. This and Plates 176 and 177, now in the possession of the maker's great-grandson, Albert Barnard Root, Jr.

THREE REMARKABLE RUGS

Sometime between 1820 and 1835 Emily Trask Barnard, who lived in Dixfield Common, Maine, hooked a rug *(Plate 175)*. She designed it herself, making it a textile picture of the house in which she was born and of her own horse Betsy in action. In 1835, according to her grandson, A. B. Root of Boston, the family moved to Dixfield proper. There Emily hooked two more rugs, which portrayed the home of her closest friend at two different stages of its building and enlargement *(Plates 176 and 177)*. The house at Dixfield Common is no longer there. Even the village of that name has disappeared. But the house of Emily's friend at Dixfield is still standing, substantially of the same appearance and in the same condition as shown in the rug of *Plate 177*.

Emily Barnard was born in 1800 and died in Dixfield in 1899. When her skilled hands made the rugs one hundred years and more ago, the old-world art of rug hooking was in its early but promising American phase. That was before the many commercially stamped patterns had too often repeated their poorly conceived scrolls and medallions.

Seldom nowadays are good, pedigreed examples of early rug hooking, such as these, to be found. Many of the finest examples have been destroyed by wear and tear, many have been gathered into private collections, and rarely can we learn who made them. But collectors, dealers, and designers properly value all early pieces with authenticated histories.

Yet beyond their family association, these three rugs are of considerable interest to the student of early American art. Both in composition and in color they are remarkable. The framing of the Dixfield house in trees and flowers, although naïve in execution, is sound in conception and honestly pictorial. A well-known artist has said of it, "Good composition!" It is enhanced by such rich color blending as comes from the close and constant association of an artist with flowers and trees. Unfortunately, color cannot be reproduced in mere words. It may be said, however, that the trees framing the distant house are full of life, the branches almost wave a welcome with their massed foliage. *(Continued on page 152)*

W. W. Kent in *The Magazine* ANTIQUES, September, 1941 (Courtesy of the publishers).

Plate 176. Hooked rug. By Emily Trask Barnard. Showing the home of her "closest friend" at Dixfield, Maine, before it was enlarged to its present size, as shown in Plate 177. Note the good composition, with trees and floral border, despite naïveté of execution.

Plate 177. Hooked rug. By Emily Trask Barnard. Showing the home of the maker's friend as it still appears at Dixfield, Maine. The rainbow, now rarely found, may have been a frequent symbolic device on early rugs. This rug is actually somewhat lighter in tone than the illustration indicates.

The rug with the rainbow *(Plate 177)* is lighter in tone than the illustration suggests. It is an audacious attempt to glorify the home rather than merely to depict a house. The rainbow was, I believe, not infrequently used in rug designs, but examples are now rare. I have seen only one other such use of it.

Simple and primitive, almost crude, as they are, these rugs have attracted close public attention on the occasions when they have been exhibited. Painters and designers, tired of the merely bizarre and startling works so often shown, have studied and praised them, perhaps not always realizing their sentimental and human appeal. They carry overtones of the quiet, happy lives of simple people who did not know the meaning of a world at war.

COURTESY OF YACOBIAN BROS., BOSTON

Plate 178. A Massachusetts rug. Recalling rugs on pages 177-178 in book "The Hooked Rug." Size 3' 2" x 6' 6".

IX

SUGGESTIVE DESIGNS
FOR RUGS

Plate 179. Uncommon square Aubusson carpet. French, beginning of 19th century. Harmonious small proportions, pleasing scale of design and delightful combination of color. Cream-colored field with spandrels of floral groups surrounding a reserve filled with garden flowers; exterior border with rocaille scrolls and tassels on a bleu de chine ground with metal thread enrichments. Size 6′ 5″ square.

SUGGESTIVE DESIGNS FOR RUGS

O MANY are the modern sources of design that the danger of overloading a pattern is today greater than ever, especially where pure copying is followed. It is, however, better to study available suggestions, then put away the examples and design without referring to them except where some special motif or form can be borrowed and properly embodied in a new design. By so doing the designers' imagination and inventiveness are strengthened, whereas mere copying weakens them, as most designers well know.

As has already been noted, some of the best designs have come from people who have had to depend for suggestions solely upon the simple surroundings of farm or village life. The unsophisticated designer often produces a design that is valuable for its

Plate 180. From an original design by C. B. Garretson, Franklin Park, N. J. Green border, black background; white, pink, yellow and blue lilies. Size 66″ x 35″.

direct simplicity, both in newness or originality of form and coloring, and in this fact we may find one reason why hooked rug
work appeals so strongly to folk of the farm or wilderness, namely,
that peculiarly in this craft they are not greatly dependent on
the advantages of civilization and special training. Nature as a
teacher draws upon an inexhaustible store of suggestion, much
of which is directly applicable to rug design. But secondarily the
suggestions in all sorts of printed patterns are of great educational
value if wisely used. Hence I have included a number of plates
thereof. These, although published some time ago, illustrate the
wide field in which one may search for suggestion and are, I am
sure, new to many eyes.

COURTESY OF MCKEARINS ANTIQUES, HOOSICK FALLS, N. Y.

Plate 181. This antique rug has a pale tan background, deep blue scrolls, and red,
pink, and green roses, buds, and foliage. Owned by Mr. George S. McKearin.

Plate 182. A Sampler of 1767.

Plate 183. Suggestive design. Playfully imaginative, but as a whole decorative. Parts of it would, by re-composing, make an effective rug.

Plate 184. Sampler with signs of the zodiac as motif.

Plate 185. Three hand-tufted, carved, modern rugs — the chevrons from W. & J. Sloane; the other two from F. Schumacher & Co. Makers of rugs similar in technique are Mrs. Lillian Mills Mosséller, The V'Soske Shops, both of New York City, and others.

Plate 186. An unusually pleasing pattern.

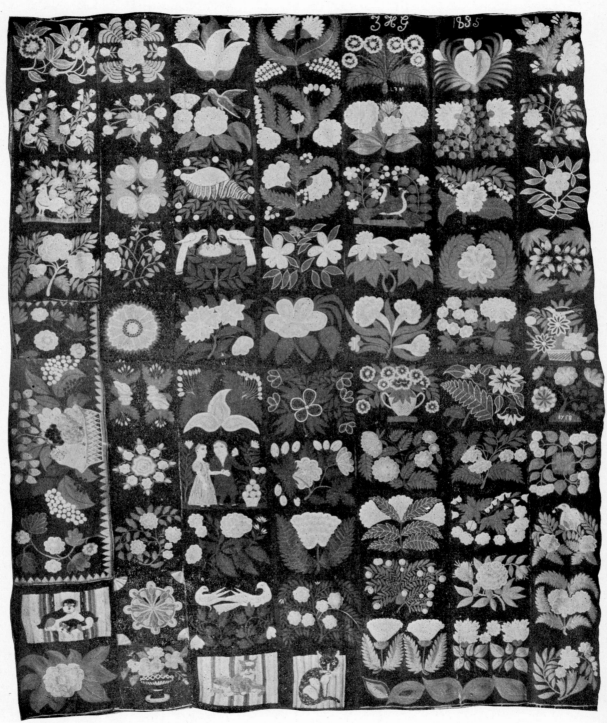

Plate 187. An embroidered bedspread.

Plate 188. Aubusson carpet of the Restoration Period. French, 19th century. A type that inspired hooked rug workers. A complete piece of almost square dimensions; center field with light-colored floral scrolls on a rich flambe ground; outer dark field as background of the baroque frame of gold, yellow and green. Size 11′ x 19′.

Plate 189. From drawings by W. W. Kent.

Plate 190. From drawings by W. W. Kent.

Plate 191. From drawings by W. W. Kent.

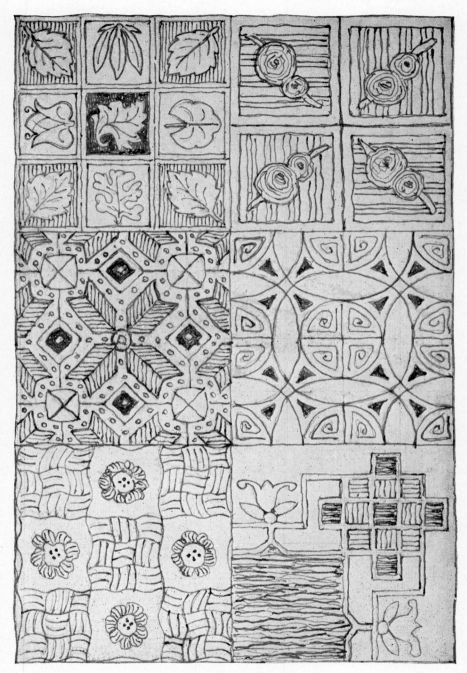

Plate 192. From drawings by W. W. Kent.

Plate 193. Portion of a woven bedspread.

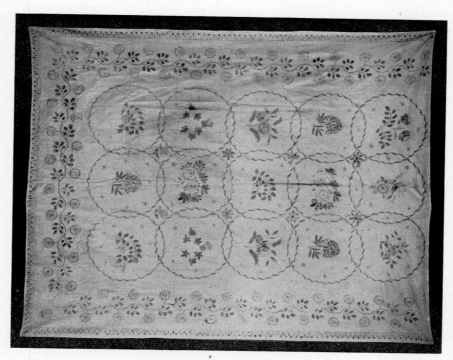

Plate 194. Beautiful old stenciled bedspread.

Plate 195. The watermark of William Morris.

X

OLD PATTERN BOOKS AND NEW

Plate 196. Old rugs from Frost's book of designs and his stenciling. Upper rug (design No. 60), gray field, soft pink and lilac flowers, 2′ 4″ x 3′ 8″. Left center (design No. 23), mottled black field, medium toned flowers, faded leaves, 2′ 4″ x 3′ 3″. Right center (design No. 45), cream field, darkened toward border, natural flowers, soft green leaves, 2′ 2″ x 3′ 3″. Lower (design No. 154), blue field from army overcoats, 2′ 2″ x 3′ 6″.

OLD PATTERN BOOKS
AND NEW

T THIS date it is difficult to name many of the earlier publishers of pattern books, but now and then worn and faded copies are found in country homes where hooking was once carried on. There have come to me copies of the publications of two or more firms and the names of others. Messrs. E. S. Frost & Company, Biddeford, Maine, issued, probably in the latter years of the nineteenth century, a booklet of many colored patterns, some of which were good. Many excellently colored rugs were made from these. But the designs therein directly based on oriental rugs were, I think, a mistake.

Mr. John E. Garrett of New Glasgow, Nova Scotia, published in 1892 a less ambitious sheet of designs in black and white. Transferred in 1929 to Malden, Massachusetts, the same company, under the sons, Arthur, Frank and Cecil, still does an important business in patterns and all hooking requisites. They made at Roxbury in 1926 the Bluenose Hooker — 8,000 of which were ordered by one firm in New York.

A most complete book of patterns, quite recently published, is sold by Mrs. R. W. Burnham of Ipswich, Massachusetts, whose late husband was one of the earliest to appreciate American and Canadian hooked rugs and to buy and sell them.

In all the above cases the booklet gave a printed idea of the design and stated the size, price, etc., of the full-size pattern stenciled on burlap, amount and cost of the necessary materials, etc., such as wool or cotton, frames and hooks.

Catalogues of hooked rug patterns have been issued by many excellent hooked-rug and carpet makers not offering to sell patterns but containing half-tone plates of their fabrics for sale. There are today many such booklets. Among the best are those of A. P. Porter, Glen Head, Long Island; Asia-Mohi Company, *The Romance of Hooked Rugs;* Bigelow-Sanford Company, New York; Firth & Company, New York, *Pilgrimage for Inspiration;* The Mohawk Mills, New York; Thomas L. Leedom Company; Akawo Company, New York. The Burnham and Porter rug products are made by hand. The others are machine made.

Many are sent out only for the wholesale trade, some are issued periodically and in colors or black and white, and in most considerable publicity is given hooked rug designs, reproduced or based on the old patterns of farm and village.

Of the earlier promoters of the hooked rug industry, however, probably none stand out more vividly than Frost. His inventive genius and his inherent qualities for promoting the sale of his wares vouchsafed for him a prominent place in the history of hooked rugs.

In its issue of August, 1940, *The Magazine Antiques* published an article by me on "A Yankee Rug Designer" in which the accomplishments of Frost were set forth. Courtesy has been extended us by *Antiques* to reprint this article, which follows:

A YANKEE RUG DESIGNER

Returning home to Biddeford, Maine, in February, 1863, a frail Union soldier of Company E, First Maine Cavalry, went to work as a machinist for the Saco Power Company. Poor health, which had necessitated his leaving the field of battle, forced him in 1864 to give up his job. On the

Plate 197. Pattern No. 60 from Frost's book of hooked rug designs issued not earlier than 1869 or '70, possibly later. The colors, red, yellow, brown, green, and black and white show (except for usual blue) the commonest commercial ones once used by rug makers, except those who made their own dyes to obtain better effects — as they often did all through the earlier period of rug hooking in both Canada and New England.

advice of his physician he turned to peddling tinware, an occupation which, with its mild but varied adventure on the open road, provided reasonable profits and improved health. A popular man, picturesque in his dress, a good story-teller, he achieved contentment and considerable local fame. To this tin peddler all collectors and makers of hooked rugs are indebted, for he became the first commercial designer of rug patterns.

Edward Sands Frost was born in Lyman, Maine, in 1843. He married Ellen Whitehouse, and they lived on the corner of South and Green Streets in Biddeford. Mrs. Ella Jordan Mason of Saco, Maine, tells of being fascinated, as a child, by the peddler's cart which Frost kept in his basement. "It had so many interesting things in it — tinware, rugs and rug patterns, calicoes, and everything." In 1876 Frost retired, was carried on a stretcher to Pasadena, California, regained his health, invested $3,000 in land, sold it at a profit, revisited Biddeford, and in May, 1894, died in his California home a wealthy man.

For some time Frost retained a Boston salesman for his own rug patterns. In 1878 the Mechanics Fair gave him its diploma, and the American Institute honored him in the same way.

Plate 198. A Frost stencil. One of the seven pierced-metal plates required for stamping Pattern No. 60. These stencils were laboriously chiseled, flattened, and filed by hand on an improvised anvil in Frost's stable. Owned by Mrs. Charlotte K. Stratton.

These are the bare facts known about Edward S. Frost, but between 1864 when he started peddling and 1876 when he retired there were eight years during which he made his contribution to the craft of rug making. His own story of that period appeared in the *Biddeford Times* in 1888, while Frost was visiting his old friends, and was reprinted in *The Dreams Beneath Design* (1939) by Pearl K. McGown. Frost related that in the winter of '68 his wife decided to work the rags he had collected into a rug. A cousin marked out a pattern for her on burlap; she adjusted it to her quilting frame and began to work with a hook made from a nail or an old gimlet. To quote from Frost:

No. 7. Large.—Price 90 cts.
Size ⅝x1¼ Yds.

Plate 199. "Lion and Palm" pattern. From E. Ross & Company's cata-logue. The same design was illustrated in Frost's catalogue and there listed as Lion Pattern, No. 7. The pattern was frequently executed in rugs.

I noticed she was using a very poor hook, so, being a machinist, I went to work and made the crooked hook . . . which is still in vogue today.

I "caught the fever" . . . every evening I worked on the rug until it was finished, and it was while thus engaged that I first conceived the idea of working up an article that is today about as staple as cotton cloth and sells the world over. Every lady that

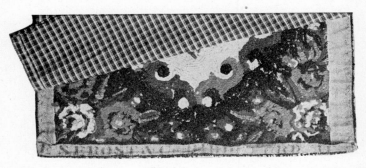

Plate 200. Frost's stamp, as it appears on the back of an old rug hooked in Pattern No. 60. Owned by Mrs. Charlotte K. Stratton.

ever made a rug knows that it is very pleasant and bewitching to work on a pretty design, but tiresome and hard on plain figure. . . . I told my wife I thought I could make a better design myself than that we were at work on. . . . I wrote my first design on paper and then put it on to the burlap and worked the flower and scroll already for the ground-work. . . .

I got orders for twenty or more patterns like it within three days. So you see I got myself into business right away. I put in my time evenings and stormy days sketching designs . . . as the orders came in faster than I could fill them I began, Yankee-like, to study some way to do them quicker. Then the first idea of stenciling presented itself to me.

COURTESY OF MRS. CHARLOTTE K. STRATTON

Plate 201. Frost's pattern No. 161. Stamped on burlap
with Frost's stencils, ready to hook.

Did I go to Boston to get my stencils made? Oh, no, I went out to the stable where I had some old iron and some old wash boilers I had bought for their copper bottoms, took the old tin off of them and made my first stencil out of it. . . . I got some old files, half flat and half round, took them to the tinshop of Cummings & West and forged my tools to cut the stencils with. I made a cutting block out of old lead and zinc . . .

I began making small stencils of single flowers, scrolls, leaves, buds, etc., each one on a small plate; then I could with a stencil brush print in ink in plain figures much faster than I could sketch. Thus I reduced ten hours' labor to two and a half hours. I then had the art down fine enough to allow me to fill all my orders, so I began to print patterns and put them in my peddler's cart and offer them for sale. The news of my invention of stamped rugs spread like magic . . . I at once became known as Frost, the rug man . . .

I soon found that I could not print fast enough . . . I began to make a whole design on one plate . . . till I had fourteen different designs on hand, ranging from a yard long and a half a yard wide to two yards long and a yard wide . . . I think there is

[178]

not a stencil workman in this country that would consider it possible to cut so large a plate with such fine figures and take an impression. It required a great deal of patience . . .

I failed to find a man who dared to invest a dollar in them; in fact, people did not know what they were for, and I had to go from house to house . . . for I found the ladies knew what the patterns were for.

The question of how to print them in colors so as to sell them at a profit seemed to be the point on which the success of the whole business hung . . . in March, 1870, one morning about two o'clock . . . I seemed to hear a voice in my room say: "Print your bright colors first and then the dark ones." That settled it . . . I sold my tin peddling business and hired a room in the building on Main Street just above the savings bank, where I began in the month of April, 1870, to print patterns in colors . . .

Frost sold his business in 1876 to James A. Strout, who continued it under the name E. S. Frost & Company until 1900; interest in hooked rugs had waned and, according to Mrs. Mason, Strout tried to sell the stock on hand, including the stencils. These were purchased by the late Henry F. Whiting of Lowell, Massachusetts, about thirty-five years ago and remained in his family until his death in 1936, when they passed into the possession of his widow. From her the metal stencils — nearly four tons of them — were purchased by Mrs. Charlotte K. Stratton who uses them in her Old New England Hooked Rug Craft studio in Montpelier, Vermont. She has issued a handsome catalogue of the Frost designs.

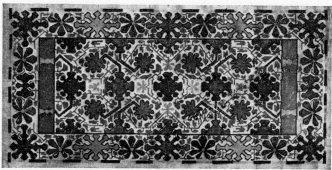

COURTESY OF MRS. CHARLOTTE K. STRATTON

Plate 202. Frost's pattern No. 124. Stamped on burlap. One of Frost's "elegant Turkish designs, copied," to quote from his catalog, "from the latest and most desirable importations of Turkish rugs. A perfect imitation both in design and coloring. . . ."

A book of fifty-six crudely colored prints showing rug patterns was issued in 1891 by E. Ross & Company of Toledo, Ohio, and a pink folder (undated) showing sixteen designs, was issued by John E. Garrett of Burlington, Vermont. The Ross patterns, possibly by business arrangements with Frost, follow closely many of the latter's designs. The Garrett patterns, which are printed in black, are largely of Canadian origin and do not follow Frost's stencils. Of the Frost designs in the Ross book, that of the *Lion and Palms* (Plate 199) has been most frequently reproduced, sometimes almost

Plate 203. Some of Frost's stencils. About four tons of these are owned by Mrs. Charlotte K. Stratton of Montpelier, Vt.

in caricature. One particularly fine specimen turned up ten years ago in B. Altman and Company's New York store. I once regretfully left one lying before the parlor fireplace of a Maine farmhouse because the aged grandmother loved it.

R. H. Gay of Waterville, Maine, has stated that H. Pond of Biddeford sold Frost's patterns for a time after their maker had retired in 1876. I have been unable to find a trace of any pattern books that Pond may have published, and I doubt that he ever originated any designs. The late R. W.

Burnham of Ipswich, Massachusetts, issued an interesting catalogue of old rugs and stenciled designs which are quite different from those by Frost, Ross, or Garrett.

Frost has been criticized for imitating oriental rugs, which he termed Turkish. Doubtless he would have done better to hold to the sturdy, simple Scandinavian, Scottish, English, Irish, American, and Acadian designs — the latter I consider the best ever made. What we owe to Frost is not his designs — some of which are superlative though others are quite ordinary — but thousands of rugmakers throughout the world are indebted to this Yankee designer and tinware peddler for his invention of the process of stenciling designs for rugs, and for keeping alight the torch of hooked rug making.

MODERN REPRODUCTIONS

Plate 204. Hooked rug made in China for Flint & Kent from design by W. W. Kent. Royal blue field, multi-colored flowers. Size 4' x 6'.

MODERN REPRODUCTIONS

DESIGN in many fabrics has been widely influenced by the hooked rug. To fully realize this it is only necessary to study the output of domestic and foreign textiles as shown in illustrated catalogs, magazines and shops. Carpets, rugs, silks, cretonnes and cotton prints here and in Europe at times follow the path blazed by early hooked rug designers. This began years ago and after frequent auctions of these rugs in New York had attracted the attention of manufacturers, collectors and merchants, the widespread reversion of the public to simplicity and early handicrafts helped along the adoption by designers of the peculiar patterns and methods of hooked work.

Some years ago I wrote to Fred J. Meyers, the well-known designer in London, that this trend of textile design suggested by hooked rugs I considered "peasantique," which much interested and also amused him. No one of the manufacturers so far has taken this title over, but I have not patented it. Who can offer a better one? The field is open. Certainly hooked designs *mainly* come from *farm* and *village* all over the world, where rugs are thus made, and this being expressed by "peasant" the word "antique," which is "antic" or "queer," covers the oddity and antiquated quality. Today this is sought by the use of faded or pastel shades which imitate the pale tones that wear and age always bring.

Aside from all other industries the reproduction of hooked rugs alone in America has grown apace. The Percellen, made by hand by A. P. Porter, Esq., at Glen Head, Long Island, N. Y., not only means superb and exact reproductions of large and small

COURTESY METROPOLITAN MUSEUM OF ART, N. Y.

Plate 205. A modern knotted Chinese mat.

antiques but new rugs based on special designs of modern char-acter, including especially hunt and sport rugs and others from designs of talented artists. Then Aird & Watson, New York make beautiful rugs mostly based on hooked and early American art. Charles Z. Gerhard and the G. E. Mallinson Company, New York, do much the same work. Michaelian & Kolberg, New York, import from China rugs that in color and composition fairly rival the old New England rugs in both copies and original motifs and of surpassing technical character. The Akawo Company, New York, makes in Japan a wide range of hooked rugs for the

American market and were among the first to appreciate and reproduce from *The Hooked Rug** many designs that led up to the present oriental adaptation of various motifs and original parts. The Firth Company, New York City, long ago made a line of "International" Hooked Rugs, many based on designs I had made. All the above firms and others are in the Textile Building, 295 Fifth Avenue, New York City.

Lord & Taylor, New York City, specialize in hooked rugs from Labrador and Canada and reproductions of standard makes. They have especially contributed to the attraction of this book by plates donated for illustration of Labrador rugs.

Thomas L. Leedom & Company, Bristol, Pennsylvania, and New York City, and the Bigelow-Sanford Company, New York City, now the Bigelow Weavers, are among the foremost makers and reproducers of hooked and modern patterns in rugs and car-

*"The Hooked Rug," published 1930 by Dodd, Mead & Co., New York City.

COURTESY METROPOLITAN MUSEUM OF ART, NEW YORK

Plate 206. Knotted Japanese wool rug, clipped.

[187]

Plate 207. Rug made in China for Flint & Kent, Buffalo, N. Y., from a design by W. W. Kent. Sand field, green leaves, darker green vine, flowers of tints of bind weed blossoms of morning glory family. Size 4' x 6'.

pets, especially strong in the hooked and also in "texture" output which have a world-wide reputation.

The Mohawk Mills, Amsterdam, New York and New York City have done splendid work in hooked pattern rugs and carpets of fine quality.

The writer has long seen the advisability and wisdom of a very close mutual encouragement between designer, collector, manu-facturer and dealer. No wise manufacturer will for long use his own personal designs for repetition, a practice which is certain to result ultimately in staleness. He therefore either has his own draftsman or, better yet, encourages outside free-lance designers along with his own force. "The idea's the thing!" no matter what its source, as long as it's *honest* and *good* work — and the United States and Canada are able to supply designers of great talent.

COURTESY OF PUTNAM FADELESS DYES

Plate 208. Old Museum Design. Drawn by Mrs. Harry King, Batesville, Ark., and Mrs. Carol King Reid, Potts Camp, Miss. Hooked by Mrs. Ben Jarvis, Beebe, Ark. Size 4' x 6'.

(Dyes Manufactured by Monroe Chemical Company, Quincy, Illinois.)

Plate 209. Hooked pattern made by machine by the Thomas L. Leedom Co., Bristol, Pa.

Plate 210. Hooked rug patterns, machine-made by Bigelow-Sanford, New York City, 1941. The one in big floral squares at back of picture was detailed by W. W. Kent.

Plate 211. Examples of modeled, or carved, hand-hooked tufted rugs from the V'Soske Shops, 515 Madison Ave., New York City. Exhibited 1937 at Metropolitan Museum of Art, New York City.

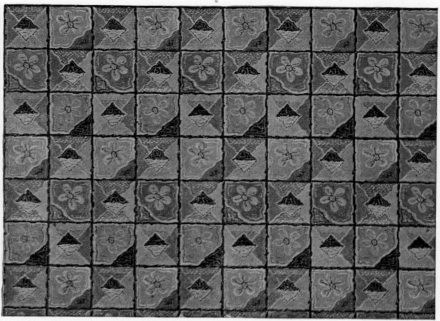

Plate 212. "The Cottage" pattern reproduced from an old Canadian hooked rug by the Firth Carpet Co., New York.

Plates 213, 214. Two hooked patterns made by Mohawk Mills, New York and Amsterdam, N. Y.

Plate 215. A "Priscilla" seamless hooked pattern, product of Thomas L. Leedom Co.,
New York and Bristol, Pa.

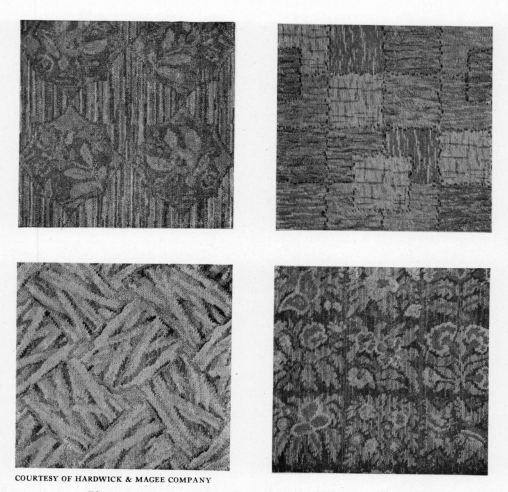

Plates 216 to 219. Four "Provincetown" patterns made by
Hardwick & Magee Co., New York.

Plate 220. A "Priscilla" seamless hooked pattern, product of Thomas L. Leedom Co., New York and Bristol, Pa.

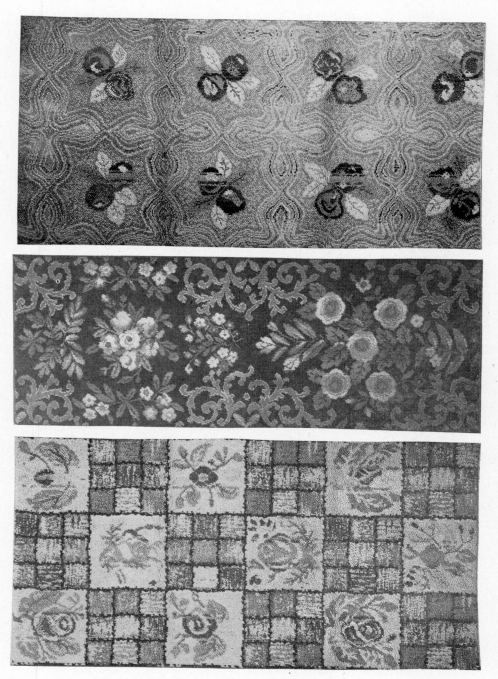

Plates 221 to 223. Hooked patterns made by Bigelow-Sanford Co., New York.

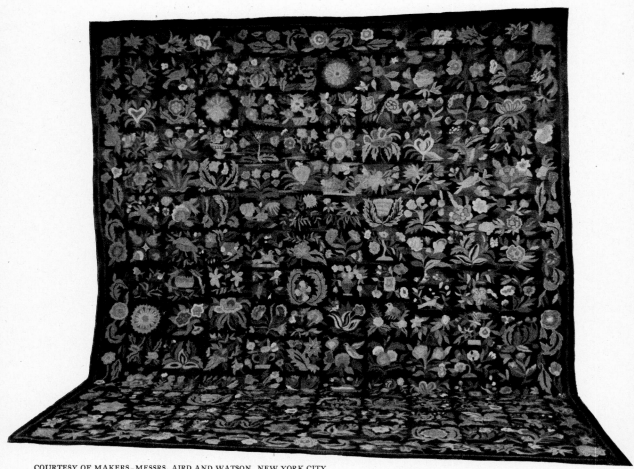

Plate 224. Modern needlepoint rug. Reproduced from antique piece showing
Early American characteristics. Size 16′ x 18′.

XII

THE FUTURE OF HOOKED
RUG DESIGN

Plate 225. Hooked rugs in the making. Showing the Rugcraft Class at Burbank, California, under the direction of Mrs. Ellen C. Gould (second from right in front row), instructor in the Adult Education of California.

THE FUTURE OF HOOKED RUG DESIGN

HAT the interest in hooked rugs and the handicraft itself grows apace in America and also abroad is now realized by all who have followed the subject as collectors, designers, dealers or writers. Thanks to the co-operation of many people and the publication of all that the latest and most important research can disclose, we can reassert our statement already made that the origin of "hooking" is *not* American, but prehistoric, continental European or Oriental. The earliest specimens of the process known so far were excavated from graves of the Bronze Age, as related in "The Hooked Rug," under "Its Prehistoric Origin, etc."

There are certain matters connected with the design and execution of this kind of rug that will bear repeated discussion because they are important for its future development and improvement.

The subject of design both as to *composition* and *color* is, of course, of prime importance, while the *technique,* or *method of hooking,* is full of possibilities as to various effects, which are peculiarly connected with hooking. Important, too, is the topic of *what the rug designer and maker can do to develop beyond past achievements,* beyond certain motifs or mere suggestions seen in early hooked rugs.

W. W. Kent in *The Handicrafter* (Courtesy of the publishers)

Because illustrations or prints from plates are clearer than any verbal description, it is well to refer at once to them:

Plate No. 226 shows a geometric-floral design of fairly modern make, but is one of many variations of the ancient theme of medallions. Herein are cross-like forms done in vari-colored, "hit-or-miss" stripes; these forms touch each other and thus separate the other medallions of dark backgrounds, which they enclose. The dark backgrounds set off and make

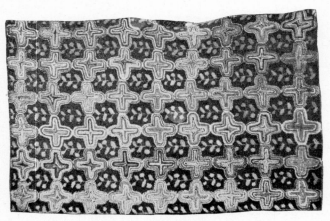

Plate 226. Modern Nova Scotian hooked rug, unclipped.

brilliant the primitive flower forms which they bear, and these freer flower forms offset and complement the cross-like medallions of a more rigid and geometric character, while the tone of the entire flower form recalls and harmonizes with the general tone of the cross-like forms. This rug has both balance and brilliancy, and by the use of *small bits* of different colors the general effect is made both strong and good. It is a valuable illustration of the possibility of using many and strong colors by *keeping them small* in scale and offsetting them by the dark background of the flower forms. On the whole, it is a good rug.

As to criticism, one may safely say that if even duller tones were used throughout, such as age does finally produce, this rug would be better for immediate use.

Plate No. 228 is an example of the effect of free floral design on a field of rather strongly defined lines of various harmonious colors; in one or two places these lines at right suddenly turn to form volutes of square shape like the Chinese; just why, it is hard to say, but probably to break the monotony of straight lines, though they are timidly introduced.

Two criticisms of this rug occur. The entire effect would be better with some form of border of a sort to harmonize with, but not repeat, the lined effect of center and corners, and if the *timidly* attempted volutes had been repeated in the central field it would have had greater strength as compared with the lined corners, and hence greater interest for the observer. Yet the design is good and evidently not a commercial or stamped or stenciled one from the shops.

This subject of fields or backgrounds is so interesting that illustrations Nos. 227 and 229 are worth study, not for mere copying but for the possibility of training the eye to note how charming are the slight changes of tone and color with almost no help from geometric pattern of a decided sort, or any very distinct floral form.

Plate 227. Unclipped late American hooked rug, colors unknown. Good example of variegated background with very free floral and leaf forms. Depends largely for effect on color and pattern variegation.

[203]

Plate 228. Late American hooked rug, from Northeastern United States.

As to criticism, the only thing evident is that certain borders would very much improve Plates 227 and 229. Variegated backgrounds offer almost endless opportunities for study and enrichment in design; this is one of the valuable suggestions made by early American hooked rugs. Another is the mosaic-like effect which is peculiar to an unclipped hooked rug. The study of ancient Roman, Byzantine and later Italian mosaic walls and floors will help one to see what great beauty lies in following the mosaic workers' lead when executing certain geometric patterns in hooking, as is slightly shown in No. 227. No other rug than a hooked rug gives quite the same chance to use minute units of color such as the mosaic worker employed in his small cubes of stone, marble and glass. It is perfectly proper and effective to use the unclipped loops of colored cloth, as he did these cubes; and by following

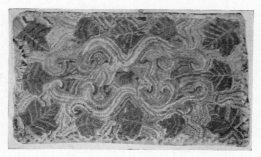

Plate 229. Unclipped late American, probably from East-ern Maine or Canada. Maple leaves, scarlet with purple and blue backgrounds. Very rich and effective in color, with no attempt at strong color.

the line of one color with another color or different shade of the same and parallel to it, in the case of both curved and straight lines, we can by con-stantly repeating these parallel lines produce even finer effects than the less flexible cubes of the mosaic produced. This was done by certain early rug makers. Both floral and geometric, or blended floral and geometric pat-terns, can be much improved by such a method of working as in Nos. 227 and 229. This also leads one directly to the designing of variegated waving, or "marbleized," and constantly changing backgrounds which, as we have seen, enrich even the simplest geometric patterns. This is one of the ways to produce the finest of color effects. In other methods of rug making it seems never to have been used, although as has already been said, the Byzantines used it so marvelously in their mosaics at Ravenna and elsewhere.

The clipping of the surface of a rug hooked in wool or cotton produces respectively different effects when matted down, according to the size and quality of the loops. In the case of wool or cotton yarn the clipped rug then has a surface like a thick, rich oriental or an Aubusson, but when the loops are of woven cloth (either wool or cotton) the clipped surface presents a coarse, wavy quality. Neither of these is so peculiarly of a hooked rug character as the unclipped loop. Therefore I feel that the more valuable

COLLECTION OF ELIZABETH H. ROWE, INC., NEW YORK

Plate 230. A New England hooked rug.

[206]

effect, *for certain uses* — that is, for the use of rugs in certain places — is obtained by *not* clipping the top of the loop, whether in yarn or cloth strips. Of course, if one wishes a rug hooked for a rather refined and elegant room, clipping will be excellent.

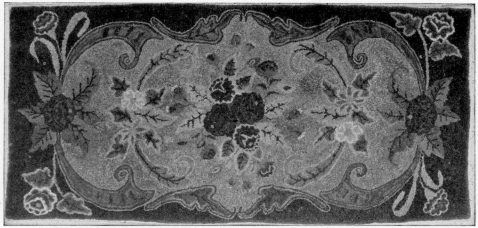

COLLECTION OF WARREN WESTON CREAMER, WALDOBORO, MAINE

Plate 231. American hooked rug from Maine. Unclipped wool. 28″ x 58″.

You may ask, why make a hooked rug to go in such a room, when French or Oriental or Spanish or American woven or knotted rugs can be made? One of the reasons is that exactly the color effect desired can be obtained in a hooked rug, and it is far cheaper than a rug of another kind woven to order on a machine. To be sure, the Spaniards do make woven rugs today of a good quality and fairly cheaply, but when rugs are made at a distance there is always the risk of bad color combinations from a disregard of the color design furnished the maker by the owner or dealer.

As to the use of landscape and animals in rug design, I can only say that both are more in place in tapestries, hangings and other textiles not meant to walk upon. Floral subjects, even without conventional treatment, are often very beautiful, and man has accepted them as not too good for his daily use in rugs and carpets. Plate 230 is a very beautiful specimen of a floral rug with a semi-conventional treatment of leaf scrolls in the border and a faint waviness in the tones of the delicate field that almost suggests a gentle breeze. The only possible criticism of this design is that some slight geometric pattern, as a foil or contrast, would have made such a rug superlatively fine. Neither the exact size of this rug nor the colors are

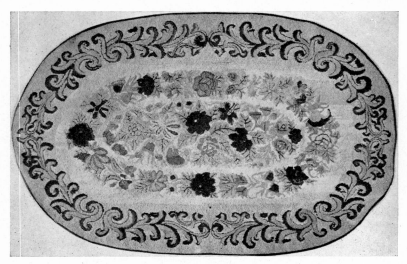

COURTESY OF METROPOLITAN MUSEUM OF ART

COURTESY OF METROPOLITAN MUSEUM OF ART

Plates 232 and 233. American hooked rugs. Early XIXth century.

known to me, but I could guess that it is about 8 to 10 feet square. The great corner scrolls are descendants of those found on early carved English furniture (see *The Hooked Rug*).

Plate No. 231 is a combination of natural flower design with conventional border treatment, and the unclipped loops show clearly under a magnifying glass. Such rugs as these were made in New England not seventy years ago, probably very many in Maine between 1875 and

COLLECTION OF MESSRS. B. ALTMAN & CO., NEW YORK

Plate 234. Thick hooked rug. Fine mosaic effect. Palm or pear form leaves (as on India shawls and oriental rugs) of a strong blue, outlined with black and containing red and black flower forms with white and black center. Other leaves olive green; flowers blue with white shadings, also two shaded white and pink flowers near center palms. Field of center oval is pinkish-yellow (*i. e.* apricot). Border of varied roses and variegated field, black and gray lines, red, white and yellow roses and white and blue shaded leaves. Edge a black line and braided brown strands added.

1885. New Hampshire produced a great many of both large and small size and of excellent design in color and composition. Plate No. 232 is another of combined natural and conventional forms, made in New England early in the nineteenth century, according to the museum placard.

Plate 235. Late Nova Scotian hooked rug. The cross is more for decora-tive than religious quality, probably suggested by St. Andrew's cross, as the maker is a Scotch woman of Brockway, New Brunswick, Canada. General effect is green, corner scrolls pale red outlined in darker red on a green and varied field. Scroll in diamond is purple and green striped on pale gray and green field. Cross has dull yellow and red stripes and is outlined in blue on a brown and green field. Very fine design. All wool yarn on burlap.

Plate No. 233 is another of about the same date in which the remarkable effect of a *ball* of flowers and leaves has been produced in the center of the design by the omission of flowers on its perimeter.

A well conventionalized design in wonderfully harmonious colors and charming mosaic effect is Plate No. 234. The shadow band is accidental in the photograph and not in the rug. There is strong but not unpleasant oriental influence in this design, a very bold use of the palm, pear, fish, or hand or river-bend motif, in that flowers fill these forms.

From Brockway, New Brunswick, comes the rug shown in Plate No. 235. Very original in cenception, and except for the cross a very well balanced and successful design. Had the cross been a flower motif it would have been far more effective.

The following observations by Mrs. Lillian Mills Mosséller of New York City, written sometime ago in anticipation of this book, state clearly certain facts which should be of interest to designers, dealers and collectors, and therefore are included here in the belief that they will be helpful to artists in general and especially to designers and makers of hooked rugs.

Mrs. Mosséller's logic is sound. Her strong insistence on the importance of signing one's work is both timely and of decided value. By so doing the creator is prompted to do his best, and the public becomes assured that the signer is in earnest and that his work is worthy at least of consideration if not of approbation.

But beyond this, signing does more than any other agent to help kill mere commercialism — it gauges and often establishes the value of individual design and technique. Certainly it creates respect.

No one is likely to help the art that will not so properly help itself.

Plate 236. The famous "Coffee and Cream" rug. This beautifully delicate and interesting work was in the exhibition at the Metropolitan Museum of Art in 1937, which was taken on tour in many large cities in the United States by the American Federation of Arts in 1938 and exhibited at the World's Fair in New York in 1939. The idea for the design was taken, as an Oriental might have done, from the top of a swirling cup of coffee with cream in it. The colors were six shades of white, oyster white, eggshell, snow white, et cetera, with an accent of chartreuse. This rug occupied one of the most coveted positions in the show of International Rugs and Carpets at the Metropolitan Museum in which thirteen nations were represented. Only two rugs were permitted to each designer. It was designed by Mrs. Lillian Mills Mosséller of New York and Asheville, North Carolina.

CONTEMPORARY HAND-HOOKED RUGS AND
THEIR FUTURE

Wars may come and wars may go, but the eternal verities, especially nest building, go on forever. With every war and rumor of war throughout the ages comes increased interest of humanity in creative work — work with the hands.

The twentieth century will have something of its own to mix into the cement of industrial progress. Collectors are already competing for the best in rug creations of today — rugs with a century ahead of them instead of behind them. Artists who never used any medium but paint are becoming stimulated by the elasticity of the old hooked method adopted by the modern craftsman, glorified to the term of "hand-tufted," and are lending their talents to this new medium — new to fine art. Such well-known artists as Penrhyn Stanlaws, Picasso, Antonio Saleme and others have gone in for what is to them the recreation of designing rugs. This interest of the great artists of today is one of the divine forces that is raising rugs again to the plane of fine art.

Hooked rugs have graduated from the village to the city, from the kitchen to the parlor, from quaint charm to impressiveness, from primitive or academic stiffness to the freedom of the abstract. Today, a hooked rug and a Rembrandt may occupy the same room. Van Gogh paintings and contemporary hooked rugs were exhibited together in the Museum of Modern Art in 1938. The Metropolitan Museum held hand-hooked rugs as paramount in its recognition of today's good design in floor coverings. The International Exhibition of Contemporary Rugs and Carpets in 1937 at the Metropolitan Museum of Art was more significant than the mere marking of a design milestone. For the first time in the history of the museum, according to Mr. Richard Bach, director of the showing, the designer was given credit along with the manufacturer. Every rug had the signature of the artist woven into its fabric, "because" said Mr. Bach, "signed rugs increase in value with time." A connoisseur seldom buys an unsigned painting. Nor should he buy an unsigned rug. One must become aware of something more in a rug than quality and eye appeal. The quality depends upon the *material* with which the rug is made and the artisan who makes it. The eye appeal depends upon the *designer* and the artisan.

What is the secret of the eye appeal in a handmade rug? This depends upon how many times the same eye has searched for the perfect rug. The average eye has no way of discriminating between the standardized and the genuinely artistic except through experience. There can be no repetition of the genuinely artistic rug. It cannot properly repeat itself in every store on Fifth Avenue any more than a Renoir can repeat itself in every New York museum. The old hooked method has been adopted by the modern craftsman but is utilized only as a medium through which art is expressed, just as paint and canvas are used as a medium for portraiture. Tradition is not adhered to by today's expert designer and craftsman except by request. Hand-tufted rugs are no longer only colonial. Just as the early American artisan placed no limitation upon self-expression through handicrafts, neither does the twentieth century designer acknowl-

[213]

Plate 237. In the reproduction of antiques all-wool mill-ends are often used. In the studios of Lillian Mills Mosséller of New York a crude machine has been devised for cutting into strips this woolen material. All colors are chemically faded before being used in the making of rugs.

edge the limitations of periods in design. Which means that all periods are studied and expressed or new periods created thereby. A twenty-foot rug in English eighteenth century, a Georgian, a Beidemier, a modern so-called, an abstract, or even a surrealist, all can be executed in the academic painter's technique with a result that is far from academic — a result that takes us a long way from a New Hampshire kitchen, if we really wish to "come out of the kitchen," or can take us right back into the old farm-house to dramatize it.

Just as early American motifs and decoration were borrowed from satin brocades, dishes, Persian shawls, and so on, so today is the modern designer inspired — perhaps takes a ride on the top of a Fifth Avenue bus and is attracted by the adornments in marble and stone on the mansions in passing and pictures the cold stone adornments transmuted into sculptured wools. And ceramics! It is here that the artist draws a deep breath of delight. A jug into a rug! Lace, brocades, Persian or Spanish tiles, old silver, are no richer sources of inspiration than the ceramic field offers. To glorify the usual, our contemporary designer uses third dimension in even the commonplace motifs, and a new idea in hooked rugs is born.

The value of a rug does not depend alone upon the actual material of which it is made, but upon the feeling, the emotion, the sense of beauty, the enthusiasm of the

Plate 238. A 10′ x 14′ rug made by the crippled and disabled in the Lillian Mills Mosséller studios, New York City. Design adapted from old Aubusson pattern executed by Frank Vanecek.

[215]

artist who designs it and the artisan who makes it. When the worker who "punches" a rug becomes machine-like in achievement, he might better use a machine. If a *human* machine makes your rug its quality will be machine-like. If interest and love of the work, as well as appreciation of the artistic guiding force within, are paramount, it is possible for one's handicraft to be raised to the glory of fine art by a rug having such intrinsic value that it even goes down in history.

What does the customer demand in his quest for the beautiful in floor covering? The following are a few of the rules the purchaser of a handmade contemporary rug should know before making an investment. Does it have artistic value? and can one compare the color tones with those of a fine painting? Or does it suggest machine-like precision? In the latter case, steer clear of it and buy a machine-made rug; they are much cheaper. A handmade article should never become "second-hand" but should increase in value with time. If your rug is contemporary, be sure that it is *signed* — an authentic signature is your best insurance of the artistic merits of your floor covering.

When rugs become works of art, they become a form of insurance against depreciation in currency and against many other types of financial fluctuations. According to Ferdinand Lundburg, "Works of art are actually an international currency, much like gold. Governments, in time of emergency, have confiscated private works of art as well as gold and holdings of foreign securities and currencies."

LILLIAN M. MOSSÉLLER

A HOOKED RUG WITH VARIATIONS

Clair Green once wrote in *The Rural New Yorker* of an original way of making a hooked fabric which she and that paper permit me to quote:

I had finished reseating a chair, and needed something for a protective covering. Being in a mood for mild adventure, I took my rug hook, a piece of clean, new burlap with some choice of soft rags, and sat down to see what I could do with them. I know some will think this too mild an adventure to hold interest, but I am sure many will understand my satisfaction when presently there appeared on the burlap a combination of loops that held definite promise of beauty and utility. This effort gave rise to another idea which works out into an unusually nice rug and is rather quicker to do than the regular hooking. Both of these styles are illustrated and described herewith, and I hope will give others as much pleasure in the making as I have had.

I seldom use a frame for rugs, chiefly because I keep my rug making for pick-up work and dislike the cumbersomeness of a frame — although one does facilitate the hooking. In a previous article, I have described the arrangement of the burlap over an old-fashioned towel rack, and this is very satisfactory for general purposes.

To make the first as illustrated: Begin about 1½ inches from the edge of the burlap in the upper left-hand corner and draw up a row of loops three-quarters to an inch long, following the line of the fabric and extending all the way across the width. It is important that these loops be uniform in height. For the second row, proceed as shown in Figs. 1, 2 and 3, putting the hook through the loop of the first row. Skip five or six strands of burlap, thus drawing the loop out to its full length and inserting hook at a point directly below the upper loop, draw another loop up through the first. Repeat along the entire row, then work the third and remaining rows in the same manner, being careful to draw out each loop but not stretching it to curl the foundation.

Plate 239.

I am confident that it will be possible to develop this method in a great many more ways than I have attempted, both as to coloring and patterns. I have tried the striped and shaded effects, and next intend to work out an Indian design on a plain background.

Figs. 4, 5, 6 and 7 show the style that I call the "lazy daisy" — although the flowers really resemble single Dahlias — and is the one I used for chair seat. This is my "pet," and can be adapted to a number of uses beside rugs, and be developed in color combinations that are charming and delightful. It is one of those things that challenge one's imagination and ingenuity, and amply repays every bit of care and thought given to it.

Leave an inch and a half margin on all edges for hemming. Decide first on the width of flower wanted; 2½ to 3 inches is a good size for most purposes, and I shall use that width in this description. Choose a strip of soft cloth cut a little more than an inch in width, and with a rug hook draw up the end at a point an inch and a half from the margin. Here make a cluster of three half-inch loops and around this cluster bring up a circle of long loops; there will be at least eight. If the strip you have selected is too short to complete the circle, draw up the end in the center and begin another strip by also drawing the first end up in the center, then proceeding around the circle as before. If the strip is too long, draw it up in the center and cut it off, rather than continue it to another flower. Next, select a bit of bright or contrasting color and with more half-inch loops, fill in every space between the first cluster and the outer circle of petals (Fig. 4). Then shear off the top of every loop in this center. The last and perhaps the most interesting step is to sew the petals in place by a stitch at the end of each, using strong thread or string. I use string, as the stitches are not visible on the upper side. Pass the needle or bodkin through each loop separately, drawing it out to the full length in a pointed shape and so fasten that the burlap foundation will be completely covered without crowding and losing the individuality of the flowers. Should any spaces appear they may well be filled in with short clipped loops of green to simulate a background of leaves.

Fig. 6 shows how the flowers dovetail together and Fig. 7 how they may be given form and shape by using a selection of graduated loops for the petals and an oval center in place of round. This last grouping was made of light flowers — from cast-off "undies" and stocking legs — on a background of clipped dark blue.

My way of working is to draw in a number of flowers, placing them at the proper distances (they can easily be gauged by the eye), then fill in and clip the centers and sew the petals in place as the spirit moves me.

The finished product is soft and comfortable for a chair seat or back, substantial enough for a serviceable rug, dainty enough — provided the material has been carefully selected — for a cushion that will stand hard usage and retain its good looks indefinitely. It is the speediest way I know of to cover a section of burlap and convert it from a prosaic feed-bag to an attractive bit of home furnishing.

CLAIR GREEN

Fig. 7

Plate 240.

HOW TO CARE FOR HOOKED RUGS

Use a *vacuum cleaner* or a *new broom,* and not too energetically.

Never *beat* or *shake* them; *only when necessary* and not *too* often send them to a *reliable* hooked rug cleansing firm.

Never *fold* a rug; always *roll* it in sending or storing. This *prevents breaking* of loops and basic fabric.

There are many good cleansers, among others are: Rudolph E. Condon, 234 Maypole Road, Upper Darby, Penna.; Yacobian Brothers, 15 Chauncey Street, Boston, Mass.; Mrs. R. W. Burnham, Ipswich, Mass.

Some cleansers pay expressage and send canvas bags for shipping rugs. All will give prices and directions on request.

INDEX